Al-Tariqa Burhaniyya-Dasuqiyyah-Shadhuliyya

Murshid
F. A. Ali ElSenossi

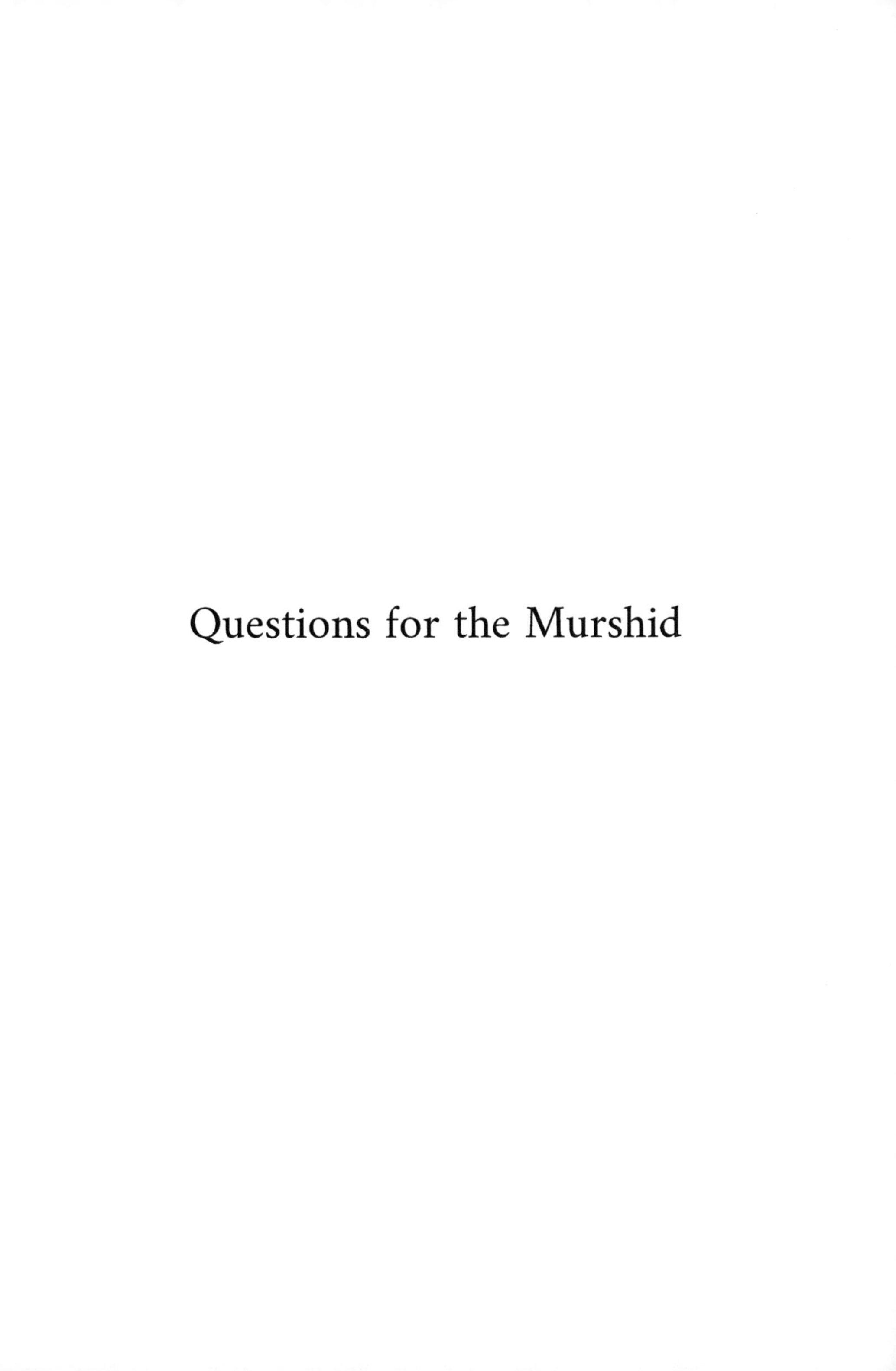

Questions for the Murshid

Travel by the Power of *Hu*

Questions for the Murshid

By

Murshid F.A. Ali ElSenossi

Almiraj Sufi Press

Title

Questions for the Murshid

Author

Murshid F.A. Ali ElSenossi

Almiraj Sufi & Islamic Study Centre Inc.

www.almirajsuficentre.org.au

Publisher

Almiraj Sufi Press

Broken Hill, Australia

2025

ISBN

978-1-7636006-2-1

Contents

Introduction

قَالَ لَهُۥ مُوسَىٰ هَلْ أَتَّبِعُكَ عَلَىٰٓ أَن

تُعَلِّمَنِ مِمَّا عُلِّمْتَ رُشْدًا

Moses said unto him, "May I follow thee on the understanding that thou wilt impart to me something of that consciousness of what is right which has been imparted to thee?"

(Holy Qur'an 18:66)

After much searching, the companionship between Prophet Moses عليه السلام and Khidr عليه السلام began with a question. While simple in nature, the encounter generally and the question specifically, as relayed in the Holy Qur'an, bring forth many lessons for those who want to learn, especially so for those who want to learn the psychological spiritual teaching of Islam known as Sufism (*tasawwuf*). The etiquette between *murid* and *Murshid* and the etiquette between the *murid* and Allah, *al-Murad,* the significance of companionship, the virtues of the path to Allah, and the importance of a question are prominent elements of this encounter. All these elements are keys that support the seeker of knowledge to empty their heart of all but Allah as they travel towards the realisation of their reality as a slave of Allah.

To learn, most of humanity requires a teacher. Someone who is a living example embodying the lessons needed to be learned. A good teacher is able to help the student overcome the stumbling blocks that naturally arise through learning. A good teacher presents the lessons in a way that increases the receptiveness of the student, aiding them to overcome their stumbling. A good student acknowledges the expertise of their teacher and trusts in the process they are undergoing to learn their desired knowledge. In this respect, the path of *tasawwuf* is akin to other forms of learning and a key aspect of successfully embodying the lessons of the teaching are bound up in the etiquette between the student and the teacher, the *murid* and their *Murshid*.

The meeting of Khidr عَلَيْهِ ٱلسَّلَامُ and Moses عَلَيْهِ ٱلسَّلَامُ came about because the latter claimed they knew of no one more learned than themselves. Divine inspiration came and Allah informed Moses عَلَيْهِ السَّلَامُ "one of Our slaves at the junction of the two seas is more learned than you" (*Sahih Bukhari*). So it was, in part, the acquisition of knowledge that brought about their meeting. In the Qur'an their exchange continues:

قَالَ إِنَّكَ لَن تَسْتَطِيعَ مَعِىَ صَبْرًا

وَكَيْفَ تَصْبِرُ عَلَىٰ مَا لَمْ تُحِطْ بِهِۦ خُبْرًا

قَالَ سَتَجِدُنِىٓ إِن شَآءَ ٱللَّهُ صَابِرًا وَلَآ أَعْصِى لَكَ أَمْرًا

قَالَ فَإِنِ ٱتَّبَعْتَنِى فَلَا تَسْـَٔلْنِى عَن شَىْءٍ حَتَّىٰٓ أُحْدِثَ لَكَ مِنْهُ ذِكْرًا

[The other] answered, "Behold, thou wilt never be able to have patience with me for how couldst thou be patient about something that thou canst not comprehend within the compass of [thy] experience?" Replied [Moses], "Thou wilt find me patient, if God so wills; and I shall not disobey thee

in anything!" Said, "Well, then, if thou art to follow me, do not question me about aught [that I may do] until I myself give thee an account thereof."

(Holy Qur'an 18:67-70)

The reply to Moses' عليه السلام question, and the subsequent exchange, is informative of the required etiquette between student and teacher. In this instance, Khidr's عليه السلام insight into the nature of the human's struggle with enduring the unknown with patience, as it was Moses عليه السلام who raised this virtue, can be seen as one reason for setting the condition on their companionship. The etiquette between the *murid* and their *Murshid* may be specific to a particular student or it could be general for all students to abide by according to their capacity. All such etiquette is taken from the Qur'an and the Sunnah for we are told the character of the Holy Prophet ﷺ was the Qur'an (*Sahih Bukhari*) and Allah informs us:

لَّقَدْ كَانَ لَكُمْ فِى رَسُولِ ٱللَّهِ أُسْوَةٌ حَسَنَةٌ لِّمَن

كَانَ يَرْجُوا۟ ٱللَّهَ وَٱلْيَوْمَ ٱلْـَٔاخِرَ وَذَكَرَ ٱللَّهَ كَثِيرًا

Verily, in the Apostle of Allah you have a good example for everyone who looks forward [*with hope and awe*] *to Allah and the Last Day, and remembers Allah unceasingly*
(Holy Qur'an 33:21)

As this verse indicates, etiquette is not a goal in and of itself but rather a means to Allah. Similarly, the display of etiquette from a *murid* to their *Murshid* is a means to, or a stage of development on, building an etiquette of closeness between the *murid* and Allah, *al-Murad*. These stages of closeness are often described as stages of self-annihilation (*fana'*).

The importance of the role of the *Murshid* for guiding the *murid* into the awareness of the presence of *al-Murad* cannot be understated. It is the basis upon which the relationship between teacher and student is founded. Ibn 'Ata' Allah stated, "Travel not from creature to creature, otherwise you will be like a donkey at the mill: roundabout he turns, his goal the same as his departure. Rather, go from creatures (*al-akwan*) to the Creator (*al-Mukawwin*)." Without the foundation of guiding, the *murid* limits the benefit of the relationship. With the foundation of guiding, the *murid* shows they have insight into where they are going. This foundation extends to all the students of a shaykh such that each *murid* is able to deepen their practice and awareness through engaging the other students of their shaykh, the awareness of which opens insight into what the Sufi students practice.

As the *murid* travels along the Path, hurdles will arise. Such hurdles are overcome by knowledge. We are told by the Prophet Muhammad ﷺ "seeking knowledge is a duty upon every Muslim" (*Sunan Ibn Majah*). Yet not any kind of knowledge will suffice. Imam Shafi'i said, "True knowledge is that which benefits oneself and others, not information that is merely memorised." In this day, information is abundant. A good question is typically not one that just came to mind and for which an answer has not been sought through available means. The *murid* has a responsibility to seek out answers. It is only once the available means have been exhausted that we can say they have a question that needs an answer. When the question persists the Prophet Muhammad ﷺ said, "verily, the only cure for ignorance is to ask questions" (*Sunan Abu Dawud*), and Allah enjoins,

فَسْـَٔلُوٓا۟ أَهْلَ ٱلذِّكْرِ إِن كُنتُمْ لَا تَعْلَمُونَ

So ask the people of knowledge, if you do not know

(Holy Qur'an 16: 43, 21: 7)

"The people of knowledge" can also be translated as "the people of remembrance (*dhikr*)," both of which indicate the qualities of a *Murshid*. A *Murshid* must have knowledge and, by virtue of possessing that knowledge, embody and impart that knowledge. A *Murshid* is in a constant state of remembrance (*dhikr*) and, by virtue if that state, evokes the remembrance of Allah in others. Such are some of the qualities of those from whom answers are encouraged to be sought.

The importance of a good question cannot be underestimated. The quality of a good answer is often heightened by the quality of the question. A good answer does answer the question, though not always in way we assume it would. A good answer increases knowledge, brings certainty, and quietens the turmoil that arises with the question. As such, a good question and its answer can give benefit far beyond that of the questioner and their interlocutor. This is amongst the reasons we have *Questions for the Murshid*. These questions were not asked and answered all at once. The contents of this book have been gathered from the almost 20 year run of *The Treasure – Australia's Sufi Magazine*. The questioners come from both outside and inside the path, reflecting various stages of human development. The answers are given by Murshid F. A. Ali ElSenossi, Shaykh within the Burhaniyya-Dasuqqiyya-Shadhuliyya Sufi Order and Spiritual Director of the Almiraj Sufi and Islamic Study Centre. Since being established, the Sufi Centre has relocated several times before finding a permanent home in Broken Hill, with Murshid Ali giving countless public talks across Australia and consistently meeting with members and visitors alike to help them gain further knowledge of the psychological spiritual teaching of Islam known as Sufism (*tasawwuf*). The answers draw from the immense ocean of knowledge that is Islam and its science of prophethood (*'ilm al-nabuwwa*).

It is hoped that with the publication of this book its contents will bring benefit to all who encounter its pages, that the knowledge contained herein becomes more accessible to a wider audience, and that it not only answers your questions but also assists in questioning your answers.

Wa ma tawfiq illa billah. And success is always with Allah.

Almiraj Sufi Press
Broken Hill, Australia

Question 1 – The Burhaniyya Path of Knowledge: Definition of the Method

In the Name of Allah, Most Merciful, Most Compassionate

Why is the integral religion (*deen*) – and more particularly, the exoteric law (*shari'ah*) necessary?

Because we are in the human state, the sole point of which is conscious submission to Allah; and salvation which delivers from suffering.

Why is esoterism (*tasawwuf*) necessary?

In principle, it is necessary for everyone, but in fact, it becomes an obligation only where there is a special predisposition or aptitude; that is to say, vocation. Esoterism is necessary for the man whose need of causality demands metaphysical truth or whose fundamental tendency is not satisfied by relativities. A man follows this way, not by virtue of a superficial choice or some pretension or other, but by virtue of a logical and ontological tendency towards Reality (*al-Haqq*); the Self (*Huwa*). In a certain sense it may be said that the intelligence tends towards the Absolute, which delivers from all ambiguities, and that the will tends towards the Infinite, which delivers from all limits.

Why is canonical prayer (*salat*) necessary?

For various reasons, for it pertains both to exoterism and esoterism. In the first place it is the equivalent of reading the Qur'an, of which *al-Fatihah,* the opening chapter, is in fact the synthesis. Now the Qur'an is no less than the Revelation in Islam. In addition, canonical prayer expresses fundamental truths and positions which man must necessarily assimilate or realise. Finally, it constitutes the most general mode of invocation (*dhikr*). It is multiform, differentiated, indirect, and peripheral prayer, in contradistinction to the simple, undifferentiated, direct and central prayer which is the Divine Name. In differentiated prayer, the Divine Presence surrounds us like a halo and gently penetrates us, taking as its support the multiple and passive nature of our soul (*nafs*). In simple prayer, on the other hand, the Presence pierces the centre of the being, namely the heart, taking as its support that which in us is single and active, namely, the spirit (*ruh*).

Why is the rosary/litany (*awrad*) necessary?

Firstly, because it impregnates us with the fundamental truths of the Way. Moreover, it constitutes an intermediate mode between differentiated prayer and simple prayer by the fact that, on the one hand, it expresses thoughts, and, on the other hand, it repeats their respective formulas. The first feature is absent in the Divine Name, which by itself does not express a thought. The second feature is absent in prayer, which does not repeat the same formula in a rhythmical incantation. The formulas of the *awrad* refer, on the one hand, to the three great stages of the Way: Purification, Development and Union. On the other hand, the *awrad* refers to the three great aspects of spirituality: humility, charity, and truth.

Humility is an awareness of our own limits and a readiness to acknowledge the qualities of our neighbour. This implies we always interpret in a good sense whatever is capable of such an interpretation. Charity, for its part, is an awareness of the fact that our neighbour is "ourself." The knowledge of Allah demands in absolute fashion the abandonment of egoism. It demands universal benediction, by Allah and with regards to Allah – "by Allah" because we ask Allah to bless and "with regards to Allah" because it is the Divine quality of the universe which merits our love. We must remember the Divine perfections by seeing them in creation, just as we must see in other beings our own ego, failing which, we cannot rise above the created level. If we are subject to the distinction between "self" and "other," we remain bound to the world.

In the prayer upon the Holy Prophet ﷺ, we realise the virtue of charity in the following manner: on the one hand we play the role of Allah (with regard to the cosmos) by our benediction and in virtue of the central position of man – as is expressed at the beginning of the formula *Allahumma, salli* (Oh Allah, send Your Praise). On the other hand, it is the cosmos which plays the role of Allah with regard to us, by its perfections and by what it teaches us – as is expressed in the latter part of the formula *'ala Sayyidina Muhammad* (upon our Master Muhammad...).

As for charity, it is the gift of Allah to Allah, by means of the ego and through beings. The Holy Prophet ﷺ is not only the central manifestation of Allah, but also the human synthesis of the cosmos. That is why we bless the cosmos through the Prophet ﷺ, who refracts our benediction – that of Allah – throughout the universe.

From another point of view, and independently of the question of charity, the cosmos is divided into three great degrees – the Holy Prophet ﷺ, his family, and his companions, who correspond macrocosmically to informal manifestation, formal manifestation, and corporeal manifestation and microcosmically to intellect, soul, and body. The designations of the Holy Prophet ﷺ in this prayer describe the essential perfections of the cosmos, while the two verbs indicate the fundamental modes of the Divine Presence. As for the third great virtue, truth, or veracity, it refers to the third formula of the *awrad* and may be defined as the attachment of the intelligence and the will to the Divine Reality (*al-Haqq*).

Why is invocation of the Divine Name (*dhikr*) necessary?

Because, as the Holy Prophet ﷺ has said, it is the best of actions. This makes it binding upon those capable of practising it. This capacity is intellectual, moral, mental, and physical. Invocation is mandatory when one has understood that Allah and His Name are mysteriously identical. It is known that the Qur'an which, in its totality and its essential synthesis is the Divine Name, is at once both created and uncreated. Since Allah created this world by His Name, man returns to Allah by this same means. There is direct analogy in the sense that man, like Allah, pronounces the Name, and an inverse analogy in the sense that man, by invoking, annihilates – for himself – this world, while Allah creates it. The voice – or breath – is the first and last of manifestations. That is why man is born and dies pronouncing the Divine Name in a natural and inarticulate fashion.

Why is meditation (*fikr*) necessary?

Man is a being endowed with thought and, by this very fact, is obliged to associate his thought with the spiritual task. In prayer we do not meditate, because prayer has a mental content of which we must be aware as we pronounce the words. Likewise, in the case of the *awrad*, there is no question of meditating, because here concentration must be directed to the spiritual intention of the formulas repeated, the words of the formula being the sufficient supports of this intention. But it is necessary to meditate when invoking the Divine Name, as by itself it has neither discursive content nor specific intention. Although meditation is absolutely necessary, it is not so in an exclusive fashion: The Name cannot be subject by definition to the thought of man. When invocation is illumined by a grace, which determines its mode and thus removes all initiative in this respect from man, or when invocation is practised in the heart, or again, when it is based on visualisation, interior audition, or bodily penetration, or on any other extra-mental support, such as breathing for example, it is obvious that meditation no longer has to intervene.

Why are the virtues of kindness (*mahasin* and *fada'il*) necessary?

In their own fashion, they transmit the truth, and because we must know, not merely with our intelligence, but with our whole being. Furthermore, spirituality demands from us something which, beyond every question of doctrinal and ritual form comes from ourselves, at least with regard to effort. With regard to content, virtue is what it is, thus it comes from Allah, like every quality. Consequently, to be virtuous is to return to our being, to our ontological and primordial perfection. Without virtue, intellectual knowledge crystallises and becomes sterile. If knowledge is the Presence of Allah in the intelligence, virtue is His Presence in the will, just as beauty is His presence in form. The soul belongs to the formal order. It can therefore only participate in truth through beauty. Intelligence-truth, will-virtue, form-beauty.

And all praise is due to Allah, the One, and only His aid do we seek.

Question 2 – Visions, Dreams, Nightmares, and the Illusions of the Self

Are there specific guidelines or etiquettes (*adab*) to follow in relating a dream? What should I include and how do I know what I should tell my Murshid?

We would like to say that if any of you believe in the Oneness of Allah (God), acknowledge all the emissaries of the Beloved Allah, you love and cherish this great teaching and knowledge, your heart is full of respect for all of the creations of Allah and you wish only good for humanity - you care about all things, large and small and you are free from hate, arrogance, lying, malice, greed and all other negative qualities, then your visions or dreams will become your transportation to the higher Divine and Angelic realms. There you will see and meet the Prophets and Messengers of Allah and the beloved Saints of Allah and you will learn from them.

You should rejoice, be happy, and thank Allah if this is your state. In this case, you may, if you wish, tell your dreams to anyone you love, for you are a real human being. What you receive is glad tidings (*bushra*) and good news for all.

However, if you are still trapped in the earthly realm and attached to the material manifestations; if you are not sure of what is beyond this physical life; if you have had a nightmarish life and demonic thoughts and can hardly love anyone, even your own self; if negative thoughts, a short temper, and paranoia are yours; if you are engrossed in the indulgence of your self-illusion - every hour of the day of a different mind – and the smallest infringement of others towards you, intentional or not is seen as a great disaster – then your ego-self is dragging you to the depths of the darkness of self-centredness. Any dreams or nightmares you may experience are for you alone – keep them to yourself, try to learn from them if there is something to learn, but for God's sake do not let them frighten you or change your opinions towards the creations of Allah.

If you put this counsel into practice, your entrapment in the earth-bound realm will have a short duration and your spiritual freedom may become near at hand if you learn, know, and understand the real knowledge of Allah and His Prophet ﷺ.

One of the most serious departments in the spiritual teaching is the study of dreams and their interpretation because they belong to the spiritual realm. This is the proof before our tightly shut eyes that the Almighty Allah has many other worlds beyond our own earthly realm.

We encourage the writing down of dreams for the understanding of the self and the mysteries of the spiritual realm. Dreams are interpreted differently according to the environment you live in, the geographical location, the work you do, and the type of life you live. If a person who lives in the desert, one who lives in the tropics, and one who lives in Alaska all dreamt of the same symbol (e.g., ice), it would mean totally different things for each of them and would have different interpretations.

For the serious seeker of truth, there are rules and regulations governing the relating of dreams.

1. If you are following the Spiritual teaching and have a Murshid and spiritual practices (*awrad*) – these practices are private and confidential, not to be shared or discussed with anyone else (even other murids).

2. Dreams are a trust given to the dreamer, a most sacred gift from above. They contain keys to unlock the mysteries from the realm of similitude and symbolism and should not be related to or discussed with anyone other than one's Murshid.

In the Holy Qur'an, Allah relates to us the "most beautiful story," that of the Prophet Joseph عَلَيْهِ السَّلَامُ. As a young boy, the Prophet Joseph عَلَيْهِ السَّلَامُ had a dream in which "I did see eleven stars and the sun and the moon: I saw them prostrate themselves to me" (Holy Qur'an 12:4).

When he told his father, the Prophet Jacob عَلَيْهِ السَّلَامُ, the first thing his father said to him was a warning "Oh, my son, relate not this vision to thy brothers" (Holy Qur'an 12:4). Forty years went by before the dream came to pass and Joseph understood its meaning.

If you wish to convey a dream to your Murshid, the dream should have the following characteristics:

1. That you feel good and happy when you wake up from it.

2. There is an intense need for the dream to be told.

If these qualifications are met, then you should write down the dream in as much detail as you can, including location, colours, symbols, people (whether you know them or not), the heavens, the earth, etc.

You should not attach a time limit on receiving a response – or even expect a response. Trust that if there is something that needs to be related, your Murshid will let you know. Please do not write a letter, then follow it up with an email two days later, then start with the phone calls. Attaching self-importance to the dream will not be of benefit either – if the dream was directly from Allah, it wouldn't need interpreting.

The teaching of Islam is a complete teaching that deals with the whole human being, from before his arrival on earth to after he departs. It is in no way like psychology or psycho-analysis, which deals only with the organic self, from the time you are born to the moment you are sitting on the couch telling your story. They don't have a clue about Being or the Descent of Being. Dreams, like thoughts (*khawatir* and *warid*), are divided into categories:

1. Divine/Angelic

2. Demonic

3. Illusions of the self

When relating dreams to your Murshid, do not include any dream with the following characteristics:

1. Erotic or sexual acts, connotations, or inferences. Any dreams or daydreams that cause the sexual fluids (male or female) of the body to be released have no interpretation to them. Have a proper spiritual cleansing (*ghusl*) and leave them alone.

2. Nightmarish dreams.

3. Unpleasant dreams.

For God's sake people – it's a spiritual teaching, not a psychiatrist's couch!

Unpleasant dreams and nightmares do have their benefit in the scheme of things, as long as you keep them to yourself. They can represent a release and transformation of the self from past experiences, bad actions and negative thoughts, and can also be a form of chastisement to keep you on the straight path. You should not worry about them, do not take them seriously, and leave them alone. They will not do you harm.

Like I said, by all means write things down if you wish and keep them to yourself, you may learn something from them, but it is far better for you and your spiritual growth if you disregard these types of dreams altogether. Don't nourish them with any thought or focus. This is the advice of the Holy Prophet ﷺ, and he is the Master of all Masters.

Good advice – Before you go to bed, saturate your mind and your thoughts with spiritual work. Read the Holy Qur'an so that the imagination will have real material to work with and powerful spiritual resources to construct appropriate forms related to your consciousness and the needs of your higher self. Our aim is the ultimate reality and everything related to the Real. We do not want to get trapped in our physiology or our personalities or our false self. We want to go beyond all of that. *Tasawwuf* is, after all, the spiritual psychological teaching of Islam.

The Holy Prophet ﷺ said that in end of the cycle, when time goes by very fast, the visions of the pious men and women contain good omens for them and the vision of such good people comprises one forty-sixth part of the knowledge of prophethood. Visions and dreams differ according to the seasons of the year as well. Dreams that have been willed or anticipated by one's own self are totally different than the ones that come to us unannounced from the Divine Imagination – that is the Real realm. The dreams that come from the Divine Imagination are the ones that can be counted on. One should not rely on fancy books about dreams by New Age and self-acclaimed gurus who have no connection to the Divine Traditions.

Allah speaks the truth and His Prophet ﷺ guides to the Straight Path.

Question 3 – What the Sufi Students Practice

Would you be kind enough to tell me please, what do the Sufi students practice and study at the Almiraj Sufi and Islamic Study Centre?

My dear friend, to answer this question – what the function of the Sufi Centre is – is along the lines of what Sayyidi Dhul Nun al-Misri ﵀, the great *'Ashiq* (the one who is intoxicated with love of Allah) and one of the first Sufi Masters said to describe the categories of Saints known as the Substitutes or the *abdals,* the changing ones:

It is reported that 'Abd al-Bari asked Dhul Nun the Egyptian ﵀ to describe the category of Saints known as the Substitutes. He answered, "You are asking me to unmask for you the dark darkness. Oh, 'Abd al-Bari, they are people who invoke Allah with their hearts to glorify His excellence because they know His greatness. Thus, they are God's witnesses to His creatures. God envelops them in brilliant light because He loves them,

He raises for them the banners to communicate with Him, and offers them the rank of heroes, imbues them with patience so that they do not disobey Him, purifies their bodies with His care, perfumes them with the scent of the people of His association, dresses them in the fabric of His fondness, crowns them with His delight, and entrusts their hearts with treasures from the Realm of the Unseen so they are linked to communication with Him, their aspirations are directed towards Him, they reside at the closest door of His vision within the Realm of the Unseen, and He has bade them be seated on the chairs of those who truly know Him."

The Almighty God addresses them, "If an aching person comes to you, feeling deprived of Me, you must cure him. One who is sick as a result of My absence, you must offer him a remedy. One who is afraid of Me, reassure him. One who feels secure, warn him. One who yearns to converse with Me, give him hope. One departing towards Me, prepare him. One praising My qualities, praise with him. Someone whose actions are displeasing, blame him. Someone in need of guidance to Me, show him the Path."

The *murid* and the Shaykh's shoes: A Sufi Story

This story finds its origins in the Holy Qur'an in Sura Yusuf.

Prophet Jacob عَلَيْهِ السَّلَامُ had many children but loved his sons Benjamin and Joseph with a special intensity and always kept them near to him. When Joseph عَلَيْهِ السَّلَامُ was taken away to Egypt, the Prophet Jacob عَلَيْهِ السَّلَامُ never ceased to cry for his lost son and his eyes became blind because of the tears he shed. When famine broke out in the land and Joseph's brothers came to Egypt, they brought news of his father's blindness with them. Joseph عَلَيْهِ السَّلَامُ gave them his shirt and instructed them to place it over the face of their father and in this way would his sight be restored.

There is a story of a very poor man who was about to undertake his journey home. He went to the Shaykh of the town and requested that he give him something to take with him. The Shaykh replied, "I do not have anything to give you, whatever I have I give to the people. You can see that there is nothing here, but whatever you desire, you may take." The man looked around the Shaykh's room. Indeed, there was very little, a copy of the Qur'an, a piece of carpet to pray on, and a few books for study. Then he saw the Shaykh's shoes near the door and said, "There, I will take your shoes." The Shaykh replied, "Alright, take the shoes as a gift from me to you." So, the man took the shoes, bid farewell to the Shaykh, and began his journey home, travelling with a caravan. They stopped for the night at the Caravanserai. Now it happened that one of the elder *murids* of the Shaykh was also travelling and his caravan stopped for the night in the same place. He was walking through the camp and began to smell the scent of his Shaykh. He thought, "My teacher is here, my Shaykh must be here." He searched the Caravanserai in earnest, looking for his Master. Finally, he followed the scent to the exact spot where the man was sleeping. He woke him gently and said to him, "Excuse me brother, but do you happen to have something with you which belongs to my Shaykh?" The man said, "Ah, you mean these?" and he showed him the shoes. The elder *murid* spent quite some time and a rather large sum of money persuading the other to part with the shoes, and then he returned them again to the Shaykh when he arrived home.

Scent is a very special way of recognising things. Long before his sons arrived home from Egypt, Jacob عليه السلام became aware of the scent of his long lost Joseph عليه السلام. He was sitting in his tent and suddenly jumped up and exclaimed that he could smell Joseph عليه السلام. When the caravan arrived home, his sons gave him news of Joseph عليه السلام and placed the shirt over his face - thus was his sight returned and his heart was consoled. When someone loves another with such intensity, an item of their clothing can become a very powerful vehicle for healing.

Question 4 – Restitution

How do you make restitution towards someone you have wronged?

There are many brothers and sisters and seekers of Truth who are continually trying to restore things and correct the wrongs in their lives. It can be quite difficult to make restitution, particularly if some time has passed. Perhaps those to whom we would like to return their belongings, or ask their forgiveness for transgressions committed against them, have passed away and do not exist in their physical form on planet Earth anymore or we may not know where they are. Sitting in front of the person and asking their forgiveness is not always the best way to correct our mistakes towards others. In certain circumstances it may also become quite dangerous to go and tell people what you have committed against them for fear of serious retaliation.

There is a way out of this situation for those who need an answer and are genuinely trying to clean up the mess in their life and genuinely want to make restitution. It is as follows:

The manner in which to begin is to start by saying with sincerity: "Oh Allah, send salutations and peace upon your Prophet, our Beloved Master Muhammad ﷺ, and upon his family, and reward me for what I have read and let it be in the book of those who have rights over me in the form of material things or sins of the tongue (backbiting and gossip) or other wrongs I have done them."

Then continue by reciting the following Chapters of the Holy Qur'an. It will be of tremendous benefit to both sides for you to recite the three *Quls*: *Sura al-Ikhlas* (Chapter 112), *Sura al-Falaq* (Chapter 113), and *Sura al-Naas* (Chapter 114) 12 times each at night in their entirety and give this as a gift to those whom we wish to neutralize things with and to ask Allah for their forgiveness. This practice is to be continued each and every night until you feel consciously (without deception of the self) that you are cleared from your obligation towards them and that the Beloved Allah, the Merciful, will take charge of this affair and settle this account for you.

For people who feel that they cannot repay the debt towards their Murshid or Shaykh or others who have spiritual rights over them such as parents, teachers, and the like: They are to recite the Heart of the Qur'an, *Sura Ya Sin* (Chapter 36), and *Sura al-Mulk* (Chapter 67) and to give it as a gift to them. Regardless of who this human being is, you will have done the right thing by them.

Anyone who wishes to be near to a Saint of Allah, let him recite *Sura al-Ikhlas* (Chapter 112) 1000 times and give it as a gift to that particular Saint, Shaykh, or Murshid, regardless of if he is alive or no longer in this physical realm. If anyone does this, indeed, he will feel the joy within his heart and if a *murid* reads this, he will feel the connection and the presence of his spiritual guide in his heart, even if the guide is no longer in the physical realm.

We live in the realm of cause and effect. People do very bad and horrible things to one another. Just saying "sorry" is not enough, you must use the spiritual gifts the Supreme Being has made available to us, the Holy Qur'an and the teaching of the Holy Prophet ﷺ, to make amends between yourself and the Supreme Creator Allah Almighty, between yourself and the Holy Prophet ﷺ, between yourself and all of the Creations of Allah, and especially between yourself and yourself, because this is where the real battle between light and darkness, good and evil, between the angelic nature and the demonic nature takes place.

This is accomplished by returning and directing oneself back to the Source of life and love and acknowledging we did not choose the place or time of arrival on this earth. It is the gift of the Merciful Allah. By doing this you enter a state of beautiful unification of the self, bringing together all the fabrications of the illusory I's that exist because of the mind and the ego-self. To live, not just to exist, and to have real visions of reality, not stupid dreams built on the stupid dreams of others, connect yourself to the reservoir of life, the Holy Qur'an. It has the power to transform and enlighten every single atom in the Universe. You will see and experience, through the Grace of the Merciful, the celestial sound that was heard by the Holy Prophet ﷺ and the great saints, friends, and lovers of Allah. It is available, accessible, and it's "on the house," free of charge. It would be unspeakable that the Merciful wants anything from us other than to activate that love and peace within our hearts. As every Prophet and Messenger of Allah has said, "I do not ask of you anything in return (for conveying this message)." You must make peace – it's easy, relaxing, luminating, rejuvenating, and life-restoring.

We ask our Beloved Allah to shower His forgiveness and love and mercy on our hearts and our soul and our body and to guide us to the Straight Path, the path of those whom He loved most. The end of our talk is *Alhamdulillahi Rabbil 'Alamein*. Salutations upon the one, after whom there is no Prophet or Messenger ﷺ.

Question 5 – Protection from the Jinn

What or who are the Jinn? Can humans benefit from them? And, if they are dangerous, how does one protect himself from them?

Acknowledgement of the world of the unseen (*al-ghayb*) is an important foundation of Islamic belief. As we move into the end times, the veils between our physical realm and the realms of the unseen are becoming thinner – even tearing in some places. These tears in the fabric of the veils are sometimes intentionally caused by those who practice the dark arts of magic and are sometimes caused by accidental cross over. These accidents can come about through scientific experimentation or playing with Ouija boards, séances, or similar games.

Mankind in general is becoming more aware of the other realms around us. Knowledge of the reality of these unseen creations of Allah, both Angelic and demonic, has not yet become general and many misconceptions exist as to their true nature and purpose. There are many examples of partial knowledge and understanding of these realms in the books that are currently being published and the movies that are being produced.

The real truth about this subject can only be found in higher details as to the nature of these creations of Allah. In the Holy Qur'an there is an entire chapter about the *Jinns*. The word *Jinn* has been mentioned in the Holy Qur'an 22 times, the word *Jaan* (plural of *Jinn*) 7 times, the word *Shaytan* (Satan) 68 times, and *Shayatiin* (demons) 17 times. The facts about how one should protect himself have been mentioned in the Holy Qur'an and the sayings of the Holy Prophet ﷺ in abundance.

If you have a Murshid, then definitely you will have been assigned an *awrad* (spiritual work). If you practice such spiritual work consistently, you should not fear anything of this nature for you are well-protected. To worry about such things is silly and stupid. The *Human Being* is the most powerful creation of Allah and we should protect ourselves with the most powerful words of Allah, Most High:

ٱدْفَعْ بِٱلَّتِى هِىَ أَحْسَنُ ٱلسَّيِّئَةَ نَحْنُ أَعْلَمُ بِمَا يَصِفُونَ

وَقُل رَّبِّ أَعُوذُ بِكَ مِنْ هَمَزَٰتِ ٱلشَّيَـٰطِينِ

وَأَعُوذُ بِكَ رَبِّ أَن يَحْضُرُونِ

Repel evil with that which is best: we are well acquainted with the things that they say, and say "Oh my Lord, I seek refuge with Thee from the suggestions of the evil ones, And I seek refuge with Thee, Oh my Lord, lest they should come near me."
(Holy Qur'an 23:96-98)

There are no tools more powerful in repelling demonic and evil forces like the Holy Qur'an and the teaching of the Holy Prophet ﷺ. The books of the People of Allah also contain tremendous formulas of protection for use in this particularly restless time that we live in with the dark forces trying to push humanity towards the abyss. The Merciful and Loving Allah sent the last Prophet and Messenger ﷺ to all of creations to assure them of their triumph over the dark forces of evil.

بَلْ نَقْذِفُ بِٱلْحَقِّ عَلَى ٱلْبَـٰطِلِ فَيَدْمَغُهُۥ فَإِذَا هُوَ زَاهِقٌ
وَلَكُمُ ٱلْوَيْلُ مِمَّا تَصِفُونَ

We hurl the truth against falsehood, and it knocks out its brain, and behold falsehood does perish. Woe to you for the false things you ascribe (to Us)

(Holy Qur'an 21:18)

وَقُلْ جَآءَ ٱلْحَقُّ وَزَهَقَ ٱلْبَـٰطِلُ

إِنَّ ٱلْبَـٰطِلَ كَانَ زَهُوقًا

And say "truth has (now) arrived, and Falsehood perished: for Falsehood is (by its nature) bound to perish"

(Holy Qur'an 17:81)

Question 6 - *Tasawwuf*, the Spiritual-Psychological Teaching of Islam, and the Sufi Enneagram

What is the Sufi point of view with regards to the personality?

In the Islamic teaching of *tasawwuf* there is no difference between the three dimensions of the human being – body, soul, and spirit. They are not different in kind, but in degree of luminations. The Sufi Masters, through the Holy Qur'an, the Names of Allah, and the methodology of the Holy Prophet Muhammad ﷺ, have found knowledge in abundance to deal with the different aspects of the personality and the self.

If you focus only on the personality, you become like the "donkey at the grindstone," blindfolded and going around in circles – he never breaks free from the conditioning and blind emulation of the madness which is dragging humanity to damnation.

The Sufi teaching on this subject is in essence the journey of the monotheist who holds the view that there is no god but God. Those who believe in the Unity of Being see the whole Universe as one single form, one single consciousness, possessing will, intelligence, feeling, and purpose, revolving in a just and orderly system, where there is no discrimination regardless of one's gender, race, colour, or creed. All comes from Allah and returns to Allah. Allah is beautiful and He loves beauty. In Reality, there is no ugliness. On the other hand, those who view the Universe as a random accident of Nature with no order or purpose will see their world as full of conflict and disconnection. We know these people as atheist, polytheist, or "those who cover the truth."

The teaching of *tasawwuf* is designed to unite the different aspects of the self and to remove the veils between us and Allah. To undertake such a task you definitely need a Guide. The ego, by nature, is self-centred and suspicious and will not let go until it has developed trust in the one whose hand he holds through the duration of the dark night of the soul.

This holding of the hand (*mukaffaf*) is a Sufi tradition which goes back to the Holy Prophet Muhammad ﷺ and the source of life, knowledge, love, and luminations.

The human, from the day of his arrival on this Earth, is learning from his parents, his immediate family, his street environment, from television, and day care. This continues on to primary school and further education. There is always a teacher in his life to take him a few steps further. If we are learning a trade, it is the same procedure – we become an apprentice until we are qualified in that particular field. The irony is that when it comes to the most serious teaching that could save our lives, everyone seems to think that "I can do it by myself." People don't want to use the knowledge and resources already available to them. They want to re-invent the wheel. This is where the catastrophe lies. The inflated ego, the conditioning of the self, stupid personalities, and the company of the no good will only lead us further into destruction.

"Give up self-direction, for what Someone Else has carried out on your behalf, do not yourself undertake to do it" (*The Book of Wisdom* by Ibn 'Ata' Allah).

If you wish to learn how to luminate yourself, know yourself, and humble yourself, put your trust in the Loving, Merciful Allah and the Universal Man, the Holy Prophet Muhammad ﷺ, who brought the teaching that can quench the thirst of the inner self. Then you will know the saying, "The one who knows himself, then he will know his Lord." The study of the personality is only the study of the illusory.

وَٱلَّذِينَ كَفَرُوٓاْ أَعۡمَٰلُهُمۡ كَسَرَابِۭ بِقِيعَةٖ يَحۡسَبُهُ ٱلظَّمۡـَٔانُ
مَآءً حَتَّىٰٓ إِذَا جَآءَهُۥ لَمۡ يَجِدۡهُ شَيۡـٔٗا وَوَجَدَ ٱللَّهَ عِندَهُۥ
فَوَفَّىٰهُ حِسَابَهُۥۗ وَٱللَّهُ سَرِيعُ ٱلۡحِسَابِ

أَوۡ كَظُلُمَٰتٖ فِي بَحۡرٖ لُّجِّيّٖ يَغۡشَىٰهُ مَوۡجٞ مِّن فَوۡقِهِۦ مَوۡجٞ مِّن
فَوۡقِهِۦ سَحَابٞۚ ظُلُمَٰتُۢ بَعۡضُهَا فَوۡقَ بَعۡضٍ إِذَآ أَخۡرَجَ يَدَهُۥ
لَمۡ يَكَدۡ يَرَىٰهَاۗ وَمَن لَّمۡ يَجۡعَلِ ٱللَّهُ لَهُۥ نُورٗا فَمَا لَهُۥ مِن نُّورٍ

"But the unbelievers, their deeds are like a mirage in sandy deserts, which the man parched with thirst mistakes for water; until he comes up to it, he finds it to be nothing. But he finds Allah ever with him, and Allah will pay him his account: and Allah is swift in taking account. Or (the unbelievers' state) is like the depths of darkness in a vast deep ocean, overwhelmed with billow topped by billow, topped by (dark) clouds; depths of darkness, one above another: if a man stretches out his hand, he can hardly see it! For any to whom Allah gives not light, there is no light!"

(The Light 24:39-40)

That is, in a nutshell, the condition of the personality without knowledge of the Creative Truth (*al-Haqq*).

So, my dear friends, do we recommend the Enneagram of Personality, the Enneagram of Work, the Enneagram of Cooking, or the Enneagram of Love? Definitely not, these types of publications are new age money spinners, taking advantage of the insecurities of the general public. Any step towards the study of anything without Allah, the

Supreme Being, as the Centre point of our activities is unlikely to be successful.

However, the work of Dr. Laleh Bakhtiar, through the Grace of Allah and hard struggle within the traditions of Islam and the Sufi practices, has done much to bring the Enneagram back to its source and original purpose. This work is a series of three books entitled *God's Will Be Done*. She has cultivated traditional sources of knowledge in the Sufi teaching and her work will be of great help to anyone undertaking this study. As we said earlier, with a teacher it is hard going, without a teacher, your chances of success will be very slim indeed.

"Travel not from creature to creature, otherwise you will be like a donkey at the mill. Roundabout he turns, his goal the same as his departure. Rather, go from creatures to the Creator, 'and the final end is unto thy Lord'" (*The Book of Wisdom* by Ibn 'Ata' Allah). *Wa ma tawfiq illa billah*.

بسم الله الرحمن الرحيم

Question 7 – Where are You Going?

فَأَيْنَ تَذْهَبُونَ

Whither then, shall you go?

(The Holy Qur'an 81:26)

This verse is from the chapter of the Holy Qur'an titled "The folding up." It describes events at the end of time. As with all things, in order to understand, we will need to stop for a moment and contemplate.

"When a wheel spins rapidly, even a wheelwright can't make head nor tail of it; It moves in all directions in heaven and earth. North, South, East, and West," a saying of a Zen master.

Man was created in the best of forms – with the potential to ascend higher than the Angels or to descend to the lowest of the low – like beasts, only worse. The Holy

Prophet Muhammad ﷺ brought the final message of Allah to humanity over 1400 years ago. This message encompasses all that came before and is the complete system of God sent to us to ensure the proper development of the human, so that he can reach his true potential as the vicegerent of Allah on earth – the caretaker of the planet, not the destroyer.

Perhaps nowhere is the human mystery more paradoxical than in the difference that exists between man's history and his potential. We belong to a uniquely gifted species whose latent powers are those of a God, yet whose actions appear to be those of a maniac.

Few of us suspect that there is anything inherently wrong with our way of life. Violence, greed, war, disaster, terrorism, and insanity have all become so common that we meet them, equally, with bland indifference, as though we had lost the capacity to be touched by life. We have become immune to the images that we see daily in the news – the suffering of others no longer seems to affect us, when only 30 years ago, the type of graphic images we now see every day were not even allowed to be broadcast.

We accept that it is a natural part of being human to be lonely, anxious, insecure, alienated, and in perpetual fear of death. There is, however, a growing suspicion that somewhere along the road mankind took a wrong turn, becoming an insane species and, like all those in such condition, were the last to realise it.

The great mass of mankind, destined in our time to suffer more cruelly than ever before, ends by being paralysed with fear, becoming introspective, shaken to the very core, and does not hear, see, or feel anything more than his everyday physical needs. It is in this way that worlds die. First and foremost, the flesh dies. But although few clearly recognize it, the flesh would not have died if the spirit had not been killed already.

Western countries are full of people who have all the material comforts they desire. Yet, they lead lives of quiet desperation, understanding nothing but the fact there is a hole inside them and that however much food and drink they pour into it, however many new cars, television sets, computer games, or mobile phones they stuff it with, however many well-balanced children and loyal friends they parade around the edges of it … it aches!

So, it is all the more moving, in this present period of crisis, that we are increasingly being afforded brief glimpses of our condition and evidence that the way we live now may not in fact be the natural state of man. Simply put, we may have, at last, begun to examine just who we might be and what we might be doing on this planet.

The condition of mankind today is more like that of the beast than the Angel. Everything we need is here. The earth has been provided with enough resources to feed, house, and clothe everyone on the planet. As we are seeing daily, people are beginning slowly to wake up to the unfair policies and unbridled greed of the few who control the wealth of the world – and are starting to complain!

Never before has mankind so desperately needed to take a look at their own lives and make some very important changes. There is a way to fill the black hole within that swallows up everything it is given and yet asks for more. There is a way from darkness to light, from depression and misery to joy and peace, from uncertainty and fear to comfort and love. There is a way to untangle the mess we have made of our lives and to return to our natural state, the way we were meant to be.

Do not blame your parents, or your personality, or your society, or your geographical location in this world, your so called karma, or anybody else for what you are.

The Merciful Allah has given every man and woman the chance to undo what has been done through genuine exercise of determination; to have access to the ultimate realisation of the Truth within yourself. Change begins with you.

So, now is the time to decide, my dear brothers and sisters, about your purpose in this life. Are you going to be part of the problem? Or part of the solution to the crisis of this beautiful earth that the Beloved Allah has entrusted us with? So, where **are** you going?

Question 8 – Seeking Knowledge in Our Time

How should we seek knowledge?

وَقُل رَّبِّ زِدْنِي عِلْمًا

And say, "Oh my Lord! Increase me in knowledge."
(Holy Qur'an 20:114)

"Seek knowledge, even if in China," saying of the Holy Prophet Muhammad ﷺ (*al-Bayhaqi*).

As human beings, we have been commanded to seek knowledge. The importance of knowledge is such that it is referred to numerous times in the Holy Qur'an as well as being recorded in many places in the sayings of the Holy Prophet ﷺ. In the Holy Qur'an the word *'ilm* (knowledge) and its various forms are used more than 780 times, and the very first verses that were revealed to the Holy Prophet ﷺ concerned reading and knowledge:

بِسْمِ ٱللَّهِ ٱلرَّحْمَـٰنِ ٱلرَّحِيمِ

ٱقْرَأْ بِٱسْمِ رَبِّكَ ٱلَّذِى خَلَقَ

خَلَقَ ٱلْإِنسَـٰنَ مِنْ عَلَقٍ

ٱقْرَأْ وَرَبُّكَ ٱلْأَكْرَمُ

ٱلَّذِى عَلَّمَ بِٱلْقَلَمِ

عَلَّمَ ٱلْإِنسَـٰنَ مَا لَمْ يَعْلَمْ

In the Name of Allah, Most Compassionate, Most Merciful

Read, in the Name of your Lord who created;

Created man, out of a (mere) clot of congealed blood;

Read! And thy Lord is Most Bountiful;

He Who taught (the use of) the pen;

Taught man that which he knew not

(Holy Qur'an 96:1-5)

But what kind of knowledge should we be seeking and how do we go about it?

The Holy Prophet ﷺ said, "Oh Allah, I take refuge in You from an eye that doesn't cry, a stomach that doesn't get filled, and knowledge that brings no benefit." The world we live in today is full of all types of useless information and we are constantly bombarded with advertisements designed to create a desire within us for innumerable, unnecessary products and services. Many of the things we see in printed and visual media (i.e., newspapers, magazines, and television) are specifically designed to distract us and keep us away from finding that which is Real.

وَاللَّهُ يُرِيدُ أَن يَتُوبَ عَلَيْكُمْ وَيُرِيدُ الَّذِينَ يَتَّبِعُونَ الشَّهَوَاتِ أَن تَمِيلُوا مَيْلًا عَظِيمًا

Allah would Turn to you (in His Mercy), but the wish of those who follow their lusts is that ye should turn away (from Him) – far, far away

(Holy Qur'an 4:27)

We can be fairly certain that come Judgement Day, Allah will not be questioning us as to what kind of shampoo we used, who won the Footy Championship, the World Series, or what the price of petrol was in 2009 (unless, of course you are responsible for fixing it).

The best type of knowledge to gain is that which purifies us and brings us closer to Allah.

قَدْ أَفْلَحَ مَن تَزَكَّىٰ

وَذَكَرَ اسْمَ رَبِّهِ فَصَلَّىٰ

But those will prosper who purify themselves, and glorify the name of their Guardian-Lord, and (lift their hearts) in prayer

(Holy Qur'an 87:14-15)

For those who aspire to follow the Path of Perfection, the Way of Muhammad ﷺ, the first steps to take are in making sure that you understand and put into practice the basic, foundational teachings of Islam.

Tasawwuf is the higher, mystical teaching of Islam and is based on the personal practices of the Holy Prophet ﷺ; those actions that he performed himself but were not made a requirement for the believers in general. The aim of the teaching is to bring about conscious awareness of Reality and perfection (*ihsan*). As the Holy Prophet Muhammad ﷺ said, "Perfection is to worship Allah as if you see Him, and if you do not see Him, be certain that He sees you!"

If you do not have an understanding of the basics, it is very difficult to develop any further in the teaching. It is amazing to see the number of "Sufi" groups, particularly in the West, who try to remove Sufism from Islam, maintaining that you can attain enlightenment without any formal practices. This is like removing the heart from the body and still expecting it to beat and provide life giving energy.

The acquisition of knowledge is a personal quest. Some people are content with a small amount, while others drink a whole ocean and are still thirsty! As with everything we do, the intention we make plays a vital role in our search for knowledge.

The Messenger of Allah ﷺ said, "Do not acquire knowledge in order to vie with scholars, and to wrangle with the foolish, and to sit in the best seats: whoever does that, his abode will be the Fire, the Fire" (*Sunan Ibn Majah*).

The way in which we acquire knowledge in our times today differs so greatly from the time of the Holy Prophet ﷺ and the centuries that followed. In the early days of Islam, knowledge was passed on and recorded face to face and many of the early Hadith scholars had to travel great distances to verify and record the sayings of the Holy Prophet ﷺ.

The story is related of a man who came to Abu Darda رضي الله عنه while he was sitting in a mosque in Damascus and said, "Oh Abu Darda, I have come all the way from Madinah to learn a Hadith from you, as I understand that you have heard it directly from the Prophet ﷺ." Abu Darda رضي الله عنه asked him, "Have you any other business in Damascus?" to which he replied, "No, I have come to this place with the sole purpose of learning this Hadith." Abu Darda رضي الله عنه then said to him, "I have heard the Prophet ﷺ say, 'Allah eases the way to Paradise for one who traverses some distance to seek knowledge. The angels spread their wings under his feet and all things in the heavens and earth (even the fish in the sea) pray for his forgiveness. The superiority of a person possessing knowledge over a person doing worship is as the superiority of the moon over the stars. The knowledgeable people are the inheritors of the Prophets. The legacy of the Prophets is neither gold nor silver. Their legacy is knowledge. A person who acquires knowledge acquires a great wealth'" (*Sunan Abu Dawud*).

When people approach the Centre wanting to become travellers on the Path, it is expected that they will acquire a certain amount of basic knowledge of their religion. This is a vital key to further development in the teaching. It is up to each individual to learn how to purify themselves and their homes, dress modestly (cover the *awra*), pray *properly*, how to fast, to pay the poor tax, and make the Pilgrimage to Mecca if they are able. The five pillars of Islam are the foundations we build our spiritual house upon. If the foundations are not strong, the house will collapse when the first storm comes along.

It is not necessary for students to become scholars of Hadith or to memorise the entire Holy Qur'an in order to progress upon the path. As Imam 'Ali ibn Abi Talib said, "Knowledge is too immense in scope for anyone to be able to learn all of it. So, learn from each science its useful parts."

There are certain types of knowledge that are required in order to run our daily lives smoothly and there are certain other areas of knowledge that we may learn as our circumstances change. So, learn what you need and remember there is great spiritual blessing in even the smallest struggle on the spiritual path.

The means available to us in our quest for knowledge are numerous and continually expanding with the advent of new technologies. There are now many widely available, good quality Islamic books, talks, and courses.

There has also been a recent explosion in the number of texts dealing specifically with *Tasawwuf* that have been translated from Arabic into English, in particular the work of Shaykh Muhyiddin Ibn 'Arabi. The efforts of many academic translators, particularly those associated with the Muhyiddin Ibn 'Arabi Society, are credited with making the works of the Great Masters and lovers of Allah available to the Western reader.

Many Australian Universities now offer students the opportunity to gain higher credentials in Islamic Studies and Arabic. In 2007, the National Centre of Excellence for Islamic Studies was officially opened in Melbourne, Victoria. The Centre is hosted by a consortium led by the University of Melbourne and includes the University of Western Sydney and Griffith University in Queensland. The University also administers a Community Access Program, giving students access to single subject study. Students may choose whether they will be assessed on the course or not. In some cases, courses can even be taken entirely online.

By far, the biggest revolution in the way we gain information and knowledge has been the introduction of the Internet and subsequently the World Wide Web. Initially developed in 1973 by American computer scientist Vinton Cerf, the Internet began as part of a project sponsored by the United States Department of Defence, linking together computers at several universities and research laboratories in the USA. The World Wide Web was developed in 1989 by English computer scientist Timothy Berners-Lee for the European Organization for Nuclear Research. The World Wide Web as we know it has only been active for a few decades years! A mere blink of the eye in the Universal time span.

The Internet is a useful tool for gaining information quickly, but there are some people, while acknowledging the benefits of the Internet, find great comfort in the good, old fashioned book. There's nothing like quite like settling into your favourite chair, cup of coffee by your side, ready for a good read. Books have an energy of their own, particularly books of spiritual knowledge which carry, and emanate, spiritual energy (*baraka*).

As we indicated earlier, the most important investment we can make is to gain knowledge of our own selves, for this is the path to nearness to Allah.

The Beloved of Allah, the Holy Prophet Muhammad ﷺ said, "he who knows himself, knows his Lord."

The Almiraj Sufi & Islamic Study Centre is dedicated to guiding others along the Way. It provides an environment where true seekers of knowledge can come and be filled with the pure spiritual food of Islam. Weekly meetings of the study group are held on Friday afternoons as a means for members and visitors alike to gain further knowledge of the higher teachings of *tasawwuf*. It is an opportunity for *murids* to meet with their Murshid, gain the benefits of his teaching and experience, and to ask questions that may arise about different aspects of the teaching.

lbn Qayyim al-Jawziyyah said, "There are six stages to knowledge. Firstly: Asking questions in a good manner. Secondly: Remaining quiet and listening attentively. Thirdly: Understanding well. Fourthly: Memorising. Fifthly: Teaching. Sixthly, and it is its fruit: Acting upon the knowledge and keeping to its limits."

When sitting in a gathering, it is always good to keep these points in mind. There is spiritual courtesy for every situation, and it has been said "*tasawwuf* is *adab*." The higher you are in your understanding and application of the principles of spiritual courtesy, the higher you are in *tasawwuf*.

The Path begins with the Law (*shari'ah*) and moves onwards and upwards from there through the different states and stations until, *insha'Allah*, we reach the Real (al-*Haqq*).

Allah *wants* us to know Him, to be near to Him, and to be a pure, reflective mirror of His Beauty. He gives us everything we need and all the clues along the way. All we need to do is to open our eyes and our hearts to the Truth.

سَنُرِيهِمْ آيَاتِنَا فِي الْآفَاقِ وَفِي أَنفُسِهِمْ

حَتَّى يَتَبَيَّنَ لَهُمْ أَنَّهُ الْحَقُّ

We shall show them Our signs on the horizons and within themselves until it will be manifest unto them that it is the Truth

(Holy Qur'an 41:53)

Knowledge of the Law and the Reality are both necessary parts of the spiritual path, complementing and assisting one another. The Law gives us our foundations and the Reality lets us fly. One without the other leaves us unbalanced and incomplete.

The great North African Shaykh Sidi Ali Jamal said, "Whoever has the Law without the Reality has left the right way. Whoever has the Reality without the Law is a heretic. Whoever joins the two of them has realisation."[1]

William Chittick states in *The Sufi Path of Knowledge* "the Law is an outward dimension of the Reality while the Reality is the inward dimension of the Law. Hence, Ibn al-'Arabi, in contrast to many Sufis, denies any real distinction between the Law and the Divine Reality which it manifests. Some people suppose that the Law only pertains to the sensory realm and that once a person attains to the Divine Presence, all multiplicity is overcome and no more distinctions can be drawn."[2]

---

[1] *The Darqawi Way-The letters of Shaykh ad-Darqawi,* page 125, Diwan Press.

[2] William Chittick, *The Sufi Path of Knowledge,* page 260, SUNY Press.

According to the Great Master himself, Shaykh Muhyiddin Ibn 'Arabi, "The Reality is the actual situation of Being, with all that It entails of diversity, mutual similarity and conflict. If you do not recognize the Reality in this, you have not recognized it. The *shari'ah* is identical with Reality ... There is no reality that opposes a *shari'ah,* since the *shari'ah* is one of the realities and the realities are likenesses and similars."[3]

The Divine Supermarket is open. The shelves are fully stocked with spiritual treasures ready to claim. It only takes a small amount of time each day to put aside enough spiritual currency to bring great benefit to yourself and those around you (for when you improve your own self, the energy you emanate changes, and you begin to attract more positive people).

وَقُل رَّبِّ زِدْنِي عِلْمًا

And say, "Oh my Lord! Increase me in knowledge."

(Holy Qur'an 20:114)

---

[3] *Ibid.*

Question 9 – Spiritual Practice

Spiritual practice is like climbing a mountain every day. It is the *sine qua non* – the "without which, nothing (can be accomplished)" – of faith. The point of a spiritual practice is to apply what we have understood into everyday life. It is the gradual adding of quality to a life. It is "the greater *jihad,*" the struggle against self-concern and self-love. Slowly, we cultivate qualities that are of service in the world. These useful qualities can only develop if self-love is reduced. To help with our progress, there is an additional practice of self-observation (*muraqabah*), by which we watch the effects of our efforts, how they are mirrored back to us, and we watch our conscience.

It may feel like a lonely, individual, daily task, yet we do not practise for ourselves alone. If by doing it we gradually purify ourselves from the desires of our egotistic self, then, towards others, our actions will be freer of self-concern and, therefore, more likely to be of benefit to others and less likely to cause harm. The fruits of our practice affect the rest of humankind because everything in creation comes from the same unity. It is scary what the ramifications are. Or it becomes an added reason to practice.

In Islam, the prayer, the purifying dues, the month-long fast, and the pilgrimage, are the basic spiritual practices incumbent on all Muslims. But in a Sufi *tariqa, murids* are also given spiritual practices by their Murshid. Some of these practices are common to others and some tailored to the individual. This practice takes the form of *awrad* - the remembrance of Allah and forgetfulness of self - through the inner repetition of litanies.

How do brothers and sisters in *tariqa* experience their practice? It is not something static, but a slowly evolving, living thing. The practice itself teaches us slowly what practice is and what only looks like it. It can be mechanical and dead, it can be mindful or mindless, it can be a ground we stand on or a place we run from. A practice teaches us what practice is and why we should do it. At the very least, it is a useful discipline. Is anything *not* a spiritual practice when one is on this Path?

Everything is, or can be, spiritual practice, yet this insight can make a practice feel like an overwhelming undertaking. Do we all feel we fall short? Do we all feel that we can't reconcile the sheer *quantity* of the practice with a desired transformation in *quality*? Do we all feel unequal to the task and yet continue to practice, day after day, imperfectly? And how are we to think of our actions, and to live with the fruits of our actions, when we are still far from having purified ourselves of egotism? This is a very big question.

In order for the practice not to become paralysing, a murid may remember:

1) One small step at a time! Purification from egotism is a long, slow *process* towards more integration and better balance.

2) We are not alone. We are guided in this undertaking by our Murshid. He is both a practitioner himself and an example of the fruits of spiritual practice.

3) Every effort counts. But it is only conscious efforts that are done with an intention of displeasing the animal-self.

4) Insight and understanding help us tolerate our imperfect practice and yet enable us to continue it without loss of heart.

5) Solidarity from our sisters and brothers in the *tariqa* helps. They conceal our faults and treat us with compassion. They, too, have their practice.

6) The example of our Murshid – a living example, straight down the line of the spiritual chain (*silsilat*) from the Prophet himself ﷺ, with his perfect *sunnah*, down the line of exemplary practitioners – is the most helpful of all. It is salutary to discover that exemplary practitioners are the ones who attend to their spiritual practice *most*. They are the ones who demonstrate the fruits of right practice, for it is obvious that they can help others, and it is clear this is help un-muddied by ego-concern.

Practice is always accompanied by self-observation. This is helpful even when we would rather not "take in" the lack of beauty in our practice. But it can also be encouraging to find in oneself signs of small changes – maybe the beginnings of more patience, or less negative circular thinking, or greater generosity of spirit. The practitioner begins to understand what is meant by "Allah loves the beautiful," or even "Truth is beauty and beauty truth." And what brought this insight? Our own, sometimes beautiful, and often unbeautiful, practice! And spiritual practice is a ground on which to stand, and a ground to return to. When the *dhikr* arises by itself, the ground is beginning to put itself under our feet. It can be a great strength. Then gratitude arises. We start to recognise that this daily, never-ending practice is the way that humans become more useful to fellow humans and in the unfolding of the Divine plan for humankind.

In Sufism, development is not only expected, but the way to develop is provided. The way to transform our actions into something more selfless, and more able to help others, is through the inner work of the spiritual practice given to us by our Murshid.

We all have to wait and see if roses bloom. And all praise is due to Allah alone, and only His aid do we seek.

Question 10 – Sufi Women

We recently received a letter from an undergraduate student from La Trobe University who is writing an essay on Sufi Women in Australia. The following is the response:

I hope that in receiving this letter, you are in the best of spiritual and physical health and your essay on Sufi Women in Australia is progressing well. Our congratulations on a topic well-chosen - *tasawwuf* (Sufism) and Sufi women. Sufism is the most misunderstood spiritual teaching – by both Muslims and non-Muslims alike. From the questions you have submitted, it seems that you may also have misunderstood the Universal teaching of Sufism and perhaps disconnected it from its root, which is Islam. *Tasawwuf* is the heart teaching of this universal religion and cannot be removed from the body, which is Islam. The five pillars of Islam are the foundations that we build our spiritual house upon. All true Sufis are Muslims (and follow the teachings of Islam), but not all Muslims are Sufis.

The teaching is based on six leaps, or spiritual ascensions. In sequence, they are:

1. *Islam* (surrender to the will of Allah)

2. *Iman* (belief)

3. *Ihsan* (perfection)

4. *'Ilm al-Yaqin* (knowledge of certainty)

5. *'Ayn al-Yaqin* (eye of certainty)

6. *Haqq al-Yaqin* (reality of certainty)

There is also a seventh stage, which indicates the Complete-Self and annihilation. It is known as *hayat as-sha'ur* (Life of the Senses).

And now, to your questions:

1. What is the order of the Centre?

Almiraj Sufi and Islamic Study Centre is connected to the Burhaniyya-Dasuqiyyah-Shadhuliyyah Order. The genealogy of the Masters of the Order (or chain of transmission) goes back to the Holy Prophet Muhammad ﷺ.

2. How many women are in your group and what is the ratio of men to women?

Exact numbers are not available, but the ratio of women to men is approximately 60%-40%. Numbers vary in the Centre itself, as many *murids* live interstate and overseas.

3. What would be required from a woman Sufi in the west to attain status of mystic and/or sainthood?

As we have indicated above, this teaching is universal and does not belong to any particular geographical location. The foundational teaching and the storehouse of knowledge is within Islam and is the same whether you are in the East or the West. As far as the word Sufi is concerned, gender does not exist. What exists is the awareness and the knowledge of God (Allah). A man or a woman who lives an ethical life according to the teachings, and practices what is required from him based on the Divine law, fills their heart with love of Allah and humility before the Supreme Being and serves humanity without prejudice will attain a higher state of illumination. At this stage, all is in harmony and unity, inward and outward, so what you think, you say, what you say, you do, and what you do will bring benefit, love, and knowledge to you, those around you, and to all of creation. Within this great teaching, there is no canonisation and no certificate of achievement. Can a saint know that he is a saint? Only God knows God, only the Prophets can know a Prophet, and only a saint can know another saint. The saintly man or woman is known by their actions and deeds and love of Allah. They will never admit that they are a saint because this would be a statement generated from the ego-self. They will see themselves as the slaves of Allah and recognise their own servitude before His Majesty and Power.

4. Are there women '*sheikhas*' in your group?

Within the Sufi Order, there are women of higher knowledge who do become teachers while still striving towards greater nearness to the essence of Allah, like other travellers on this path of illumination. Within our Order, there are also saintly women named in the chain of transmission (*silsilat*).

Do we have '*sheikhas*' in our Sufi Order? In the real meaning of the word, no, we do not.

5. Do you think it possible that a western woman Sufi saint from a western Sufi order would or could be accepted by mainstream Islam?

Based on the definition of *tasawwuf* that we have spoken of, the simple answer to your question is yes. Sainthood is between Allah and His slave. If the individual has been accepted by Allah as His Friend and by those who are near (*muqarrabun*), recognition of their sainthood by the community is not an issue. There are such women who exist within the Muslim world and have attained a status of tremendous respect and honour because of their saintliness, their knowledge of the teaching, and their ability to touch the hearts of others with the Divine teaching of Islam, both inward and outward. Acceptance is put on earth by the Divine favour for those who are chosen by the Beloved Allah, whether they be male or female.

6. Are there any women in your organization who are ascetics – choosing to practice their faith without being wives, mothers, or in the workforce?

Tasawwuf is the Divine Ocean of all human beings - from a child of one year to a man or woman of 100 years old or greater. Their occupations, qualifications, marital status, and whether they have children or not is up to Allah. If they can swim in the Divine Ocean, then they are part of the path. Being married or single, rich or poor, these are transitory conditions, and in our organisation we have all kinds; wives, mothers, students, business women and ascetics.

We wish you success in your studies and hope that the answers we have provided will bring you benefit.

Question 11 – Books on Sufism

Can you please recommend some books on *tasawwuf* which actually detail the method and the stages of the journey and not just the concepts?

My dear brother, I am writing this email to you in response to your query: "I am new to the subject of *tasawwuf*." Let me say this to you, for our Beloved Allah to raise your awareness and consciousness and your belief (*iman*) to enquire about the most powerful teaching in the universe and within Islam is a very great and tremendous blessing. *Tasawwuf* is the heart of Islam and no one book will ever be able to answer the mystery of life, existence, and the Supreme Being, Almighty Allah, all Glory be to Him, except one book and that is the Holy Qur'an, the word of Allah. To unlock the mysteries of the Revelations and the secrets of this book will take thousands of years.

The Qur'an itself, from the time it has been revealed to our Beloved Prophet ﷺ, the Seal of the Messengers, is still in the process of unfolding. The revelation is complete in the Holy Qur'an and the Hadith. However, the unveiling of the knowledge contained within will never end, because the end is with Allah and Allah has no end. It has been said that within every verse in the Holy Qur'an there are 70,000 meanings. And Sayyiduna Ali ibn Abi Talib ﵁ has said, "If the Holy Prophet ﷺ permitted me, I would load 70 camels with books to explain the opening chapter of the Holy Qur'an (*Sura al-Fatihah*)."

However, I have put together a collection of books for you to help you get started and to open the inner eye of your heart and to give you the tools and the understanding of how to unveil the mysteries of Allah. The aim is to reach the reality of, as the Holy Prophet ﷺ said, "Whoever knows himself, will know his Lord." The connection is so powerful when we become conscious and aware and no longer in a state of sleep or forgetfulness (*ghafla*). I am absolutely sure that if you take the necessary steps to absorb the teaching contained within these books, you will find yourself in a different world altogether. It is a small sacrifice to make for spiritual attainment, but as the saying goes "you can lead ... but you cannot make him drink." This is totally up to you and your determination and your sincerity.

I supplicate to my Beloved Allah, through the Grace of our Beloved Holy Prophet ﷺ, to illuminate your heart and mind and to guide us to His Presence. After everything is said and done, Allah told us:

وَفِيٓ أَنفُسِكُمۡۚ أَفَلَا تُبۡصِرُونَ

And it is within you, can you not see?
(Holy Qur'an 51:21)

Recommended Reading

The Holy Qur'an, translation by Abdullah Yusuf Ali

Sahih Bukhari

Muhammad: His Life Based on the Earliest Sources, Martin Lings

Fat-Hud Dayyan Fi Fighi Khairil Adyan: Opening towards understanding the Best of Religions, Muhammad Ibn Ahmad Lebbai

Islam: Beliefs and Teachings, Ghulam Sarwar

The Language of the Future: Book of Sufi Terminology, Murshid F.A. Ali ElSenossi

Kashf al-Mahjub: Unveiling the Veiled, Syed Ali bin Uthman al-Hujweri

Sufi Book of Spiritual Ascent: al-Risala al-Qushayriyya, Abu'l-Qasim al-Qushayri

The Book of Sufi Healing, Shaykh Chishti

Realities of Sufism, Shaykh 'Abd al-Qadir 'Isa

Irshad: Wisdom of a Sufi Master, Sheikh Muzaffer Ozak al-Jerrahi

Sufism - A Beginners Guide, William Chittick

The Sufi Path of Knowledge, William Chittick

What is Sufism?, Martin Lings

An Introduction to Sufism, Titus Burckhardt

The Vision of Islam, Sachiko Murata and William Chittick

Question 12 – Gifts in Islam

What is the proper way to give and receive a gift according to the teaching of the Holy Prophet ﷺ?

آمِنُوا بِاللَّهِ وَرَسُولِهِ وَأَنفِقُوا مِمَّا جَعَلَكُم مُّسْتَخْلَفِينَ فِيهِ
فَالَّذِينَ آمَنُوا مِنكُمْ وَأَنفَقُوا لَهُمْ أَجْرٌ كَبِيرٌ

Believe in Allah and His messenger, and spend of that whereof He has made you trustees; and such of you as believe and spend (rightly), theirs will be a great reward
(Holy Qur'an 57:7)

Narrated from Asma, the Messenger of Allah ﷺ said, "Give and do not give reluctantly lest Allah should give you in a limited amount; and do not withhold your money lest Allah should withhold it from you" (*Sahih Bukhari*).

The *Adab* of the Giver

We should realise the one who is receiving our gift is doing us the honour of accepting our offering. This same principle applies when we invite someone to our homes to share a meal with us. We should be grateful to them for relieving us of the responsibility of holding what was destined to come to them from Allah. We should show thanks and gratitude to them for receiving our gift, for if we are not thankful towards our fellow man, we are not thankful towards Allah.

The giver should make little of his offering, even if it were the size of a mountain, so that the receiver does not feel an obligation towards them. There should never be any strings attached to a gift. In the western world, we seem to have a rule that a gift cannot be passed on, that we are somehow obligated to keep it forever (and make sure that it is on display when the giver comes to visit). If this is the case, then it was not really a gift in the first place. In reality, it is the essence of the gift which stays with us. The spirit in which the gift was given is ours alone and stays with us always.

The *Adab* of the Receiver

When receiving a gift, one should treat it with respect and show happiness, even if the gift is very small or you are not in need of it. Keep in mind the feelings and intent of the giver and accept the gift graciously so as not to cause discomfort or hurt to the one offering the gift.

One should make *dua'* for the giver, asking for Allah's blessings upon them, even if they are absent (for example by saying *MaSha'Allah* or *Jazzak Allah al-khair* – Glory be to Allah and may Allah reward you well). The Holy Prophet ﷺ said, "if you say this to anyone, then you have thanked him more than is required."

One should receive the gift with grace and a smile if the giver is present, looking for the opportunity to reciprocate sometime in the future.

One should thank him and appreciate what he has done, sharing the gift with the giver if practical.

One should not allow oneself to become subjugated to the giver.

And be careful – do not lose your faith with it as well – remove the desire to receive more.

The spirit of giving and receiving changes when one comes to realise that the force behind our intent to give and our ability to receive, is none other than Allah. Everything comes from Allah and to Him is our return.

We should perform all our actions of giving and receiving with the realisation that everything belongs to Allah, that we are merely trustees for Allah and, like anything else, we will be responsible with regard to the disposition of this trust.

Question 13 – Sincerity

You have spoken many times about sincerity. Using an example from the Life of the Holy Prophet ﷺ would you please explain to us what this really means? We understand that it is the key to the teaching of Islam.

This hadith of the Holy Prophet ﷺ covers the question you have asked and gives beautiful and serious answers to achieve spiritual success. It is related by Abu Kabshah al-Ammari رضي الله عنه that he heard the Messenger of Allah ﷺ say, "There are three things for which I can swear and, in addition to them, there is another thing that I want to tell you. So, remember it. The three things for which I can swear are:

1. No one will become poor by spending in the Way of Allah (Allah will bestow prosperity on him and multiply his wealth).

2. Injustice will not be done to a bondsman but that Allah will raise him in esteem in return for it (For example, when a wrong is perpetrated on a person and he bears it patiently, Allah will cause an increase in his high rank and good reputation).

3. No one will open the door of begging, but Allah will open the door of poverty for him (whoever will make it his habit to extend a begging hand towards others will be condemned to want and indigence by Allah).

The thing that I want to tell you and which you should remember, apart from these, is that this world is for four types of men.

1. The slave whom Allah has granted wealth as well as the knowledge of the correct way of life. They fear Allah in the expenditure and utilisation of their goods, show kindness to relatives by means of them, and spend them in the way it ought to be done for the good pleasure of the Lord. These persons are of the highest grade.

2. The slave whom Allah has endowed with correct knowledge and the right spirit but has not given them wealth. Their intention is sound, and they honestly feel and say that if they come into wealth, they too will spend and utilise it as such and such a virtuous man does. The recompense of both these types of men is equal (people of the second category will be rewarded in the same way as those of the first due to the purity of their intention).

3. The slave to whom Allah gave wealth but not the knowledge and spirit of using and spending it properly. They spend their goods foolishly, in wrong ways and without the fear of Allah, do not show kindness to relatives through their worldly possessions, nor spend them as they ought to be spent. These are the worst kind of men.

4. The slave whom Allah gave neither wealth nor right knowledge and spirit. They say that if they obtain wealth, they, too, will spend it as such and such a wasteful and self-indulgent man does. Such is their intention and the sin of both these types of men is equal (the fault of the people of the last category will be identical, due to their evil

intention, to what is of the people belonging to the third category owing to their misdeeds)" (*Jami' al-Tirmidhi*).

And Allah says in His Holy Book:

إِنَّمَا الْمُؤْمِنُونَ الَّذِينَ آمَنُوا بِاللَّهِ وَرَسُولِهِ ثُمَّ لَمْ يَرْتَابُوا وَجَاهَدُوا بِأَمْوَالِهِمْ وَأَنفُسِهِمْ فِي سَبِيلِ اللَّهِ أُولَئِكَ هُمُ الصَّادِقُونَ

Only those are Believers who have believed in Allah and His Messenger, and have never since doubted, but have striven with their belongings and their persons in the Cause of Allah: Such are the sincere ones

(Holy Qur'an 49:15)

Question 14 – Perfection

Our Beloved Allah has said in the Holy Qur'an:

وَمَا خَلَقْتُ ٱلْجِنَّ وَٱلْإِنسَ إِلَّا لِيَعْبُدُونِ

I have not created the invisible beings and men to any end other than that they may [know and] worship Me
(Holy Qur'an 51:56)

The teacher of all, the Seal of all Emissaries, the Holy Prophet Muhammad ﷺ, is the last miracle the Supreme Being has given to the creations and he has said "Seek knowledge from the cradle to the grave."

The totality of the teaching of the Holy Prophet ﷺ – the *ahadith* and the Holy Qur'an, the only miracle available to humanity in particular and to the rest of the creations in general, contain questions and answers. If the eye of your heart is open, then you don't have to go too far to find your answers. As the saying tells us "knowledge is (to be found) in the heart, not in printed materials." But it is like finding diamonds in the Earth, you have to roll up your sleeves and do a bit of work in order to bring out the treasure.

يَٰٓأَيُّهَا ٱلنَّاسُ إِنَّا خَلَقْنَٰكُم مِّن ذَكَرٍ وَأُنثَىٰ وَجَعَلْنَٰكُمْ
شُعُوبًا وَقَبَآئِلَ لِتَعَارَفُوٓا۟ إِنَّ أَكْرَمَكُمْ عِندَ ٱللَّهِ أَتْقَىٰكُمْ إِنَّ
ٱللَّهَ عَلِيمٌ خَبِيرٌ

O mankind! Behold, We have created you all out of a male and a female, and have made you into nations and tribes, so that you might come to know one another. Verily, the noblest of you in the sight of God is the one who is most deeply conscious of Him. Behold, God is All-Knowing, All-Aware

(Holy Qur'an 49:13)

A man asked one of the Companions of the Holy Prophet ﷺ, "Do you see God?" and he answered, "I will not worship anything that I cannot see." The Holy Prophet ﷺ said,

"Worship Allah as if you see Him and if you cannot see him, you must know that He sees you" (*Sunan al-Nasa'i*).

One of our kind sisters has raised a question concerning the difference between a man of devotion and a man of knowledge and which one is more perfect. Devotion is *'ibadah,* or worship, and this is the realm of the *'abid,* the worshipper. *'Ilm* is knowledge, and the *'alim* encompasses both, as the *'alim* must also be man of devotion. As the Holy Prophet ﷺ has said, "Whoever acts upon what he knows, Allah will give him the knowledge of that which he does not know." And, "The angels will lower their wings in their great pleasure with one who seeks knowledge; the inhabitants of the heavens and the earth and the fish in the deep waters will ask forgiveness for the learned man. The superiority of the learned man over the devout worshipper is like that of the moon, on the night when it is full, over the rest of the stars" (*Sunan Abu Dawud*).

The teaching of Allah, from the very beginning of creation, deals with knowledge. The great one among the Jinn objected to the command of Allah to prostrate to Adam by saying "I am better than him" (Holy Qur'an 7:12). These words are still with us up to now. Pride and arrogance are veils that keep us from accessing the true knowledge that is within us.

Even the *'arif* has to eventually let go of his *ma'rifa* – His knowledge of Allah is a veil which blocks his witnessing of the Divine Presence. All things spiritual that we practice in any form or shape are a means to the end, not the end-in-itself. The end is beyond all that we could imagine. Our great Saints of Allah have a saying, *"laa ya'arif Allah, il Allah"* (No one knows Allah, except Allah). In the activities of our daily lives there are some things that we can do and there are limitless things that we have no control or power over. We cannot command the sun to rise at midnight or tell the celestial spheres to reshuffle themselves or to align themselves according to our own desires.

For this reason, we have to look seriously at how we arrived on planet Earth. Did we make a booking and reserve a seat on the Divine airplane? Did we travel first class? Did we choose our destination or the family we were born into? Did we come prepared with all that is required from us to exist on our transitory stopover? The miracle of life teaches us about life. We exit the womb of our mothers totally helpless and dependent and we stay in that condition until we reach the age of physical maturity, yet we remain totally in need of the Divine help all throughout our lives. From before the first breath we take until the last breath we exhale we are in a state of learning. The Holy Prophet ﷺ said, "Seek knowledge from the cradle to the grave." And our Beloved Allah has said, "Above everyone who knows, there is someone who knows more" (*Hadith Qudsi*). When you open the pages of the Holy Qur'an, one of the only things He said to ask for more of is knowledge.

وَقُل رَّبِّ زِدْنِي عِلْمًا

And say, "Oh my Lord! Increase me in knowledge."

(Holy Qur'an 20:114)

We are living in the end of the cycle, and it is like any other end, things are upside down and backwards. We now encounter the variations of the different levels of human beings daily. "The one who knows and knows that he knows, he is an *'alim,* learn from him. The one who knows and does not know that he knows; is a sleeping teacher, awaken him and learn from him. The one who does not know and knows that he does not know, is a seeker of truth, teach him - and the one who does not know and does not know that he does not know; is a fool, run from him."

The Holy Prophet 'Isa عَلَيْهِ ٱلسَّلَامُ once ran past a man shouting, "Run, run for your lives." The man ran along with him, asking, "Is there an army chasing you?" "Worse than that," he replied. "A wild animal?" the man asked. "No, no, much worse than that," replied the Prophet عَلَيْهِ ٱلسَّلَامُ. The man said to him, "Oh, Spirit of God, what then are you running from?" "I am running from the fools," he replied. The man was even more surprised, for he knew that Jesus عَلَيْهِ ٱلسَّلَامُ was a prophet. He had cured the sick and brought the dead back to life. So, he said, "But 'Isa, you have power to bring the dead to life." Prophet 'Isa عَلَيْهِ ٱلسَّلَامُ smiled and said, "True, I have healed the sick and brought the dead to life, but it is nearly impossible to bring a fool to his senses."

If we really look at what is happening in the world today, we will run away even faster than the Holy Prophet 'Isa, son of Mary. We live in an age of "consumer spirituality," where spiritual teachings are chosen from a menu, learned over the course of a weekend, and then passed on to others. Everyone thinks themselves to be a great teacher and the only one who knows the ultimate truth. There are even those who do not shy away from declaring themselves (and everyone else) to be God, without so much as the blink of an eye.

The website of one Guru declares that she follows no particular religion and that to achieve enlightenment on her path there are no rules to follow. She has, of course, many admirers as demonstrated by the throngs of Australians who attended recent meetings, but also more than a few detractors, one of which called her a "spiritual vampire" sucking the life force and energy out of those who connected themselves to her. Unfortunately, there are many foolish people who willingly allow themselves to be misguided.

In this age and time, if we have even the smallest ailment, we look for a qualified practitioner to assist us in healing, so that the medication we are given will be the right one for us. It should be so much more so with regards to our spiritual health.

There are three types of knowledge: Knowledge of the Spirit, which the Loving Creator has given to all but hidden from us, and Knowledge of the Soul which is closely connected to Knowledge of the Physical-Self. One may live and die without uncovering the Knowledge of the Spirit because of the state of forgetfulness we live in. We busy ourselves working to feed and groom the body and using the energies of the Soul, which is a defence mechanism of the Ego to prevent development from occurring. This type of life is below that of the animal-self.

So, let's cut to the chase. This advice is for myself and for whoever reads these few lines printed on paper: First, there was nothing, only the Supreme Being, the Almighty, the Merciful Allah. Then, He created the creations. From the moment we arrive on Earth, we are being provided for by

Him – and we belong to Him. We have been given a certain period of time to make business with the Creator. He has said:

إِنَّ ٱللَّهَ ٱشْتَرَىٰ مِنَ ٱلْمُؤْمِنِينَ أَنفُسَهُمْ وَأَمْوَٰلَهُمْ

Allah has purchased of the believers their persons and their goods

(Holy Qur'an 9:111)

This covers everyone, because everyone is a believer, whether he believes in Allah, or he believes in the creations of Allah. The sorting out will be on the Day of Reckoning and is in the hands of Allah alone. Everything in the material world, the ideas and their development, the benefit that we receive, and the misery that we can cause with new technologies, is all a test. One path will take you on the Divine freeway - you will arrive safely, full of illumination and knowledge and full of love. Love looks for love and Allah has said:

فَسَوْفَ يَأْتِى ٱللَّهُ بِقَوْمٍ يُحِبُّهُمْ وَيُحِبُّونَهُۥ

He will produce a people whom He will love as they will love Him

(Holy Qur'an 5:54)

One should not waste the precious time, the golden opportunity that Allah, the Wise (*al-Hakim*), has given us. Knowledge is abundant, ready to be claimed. The false Messiah and teachers without credentials, who possess only articles and references to books and references to references, put limitations on knowledge that has no limit; they are like "the blind leading the blind" or "the sick leaning on the dead."

So, we should work on opening the eye of our hearts, but, to be a great worshipper or a great *'alim* or a great *'arif,* or whatever 'greatness' you are or want to be - remember how you arrived and how you will be leaving this place. And remember that greatness comes from the Great, the Creator of all things and is not of your own creation. The key to the success of every human being is not in how much you know, or how much you practice, it is the purification of the heart that is essential. To purify one's heart and to cleanse it in such a way that it will become fit for the King of all Kings to take up His rightful place is the ultimate aim. Then, you will learn humbleness, kindness, and many other wonderful things will be given to you as well. The Holy Prophet ﷺ said, "When Allah discloses Himself to a thing, it humbles itself to Him" (*Sunan Ibn Majah*). And that will bring our lives to a state of peace. The key and the secret behind the key is that you will *know* with absolute certainty that you are *faqir*, poor, and if you understand this formula, all the answers will come rushing to your consciousness and they will polish your spiritual heart, removing the false lenses, the false ideas and your spiritual ears will be like the greatest satellite dish ever created. They will hear the celestial sound of:

يَٰٓأَيُّهَا ٱلنَّاسُ أَنتُمُ ٱلْفُقَرَآءُ إِلَى ٱللَّهِ وَٱللَّهُ هُوَ ٱلْغَنِىُّ ٱلْحَمِيدُ

O mankind! It is you who are poor towards Allah, whereas He alone is self-sufficient, the One to whom all praise is due

(Holy Qur'an 35:15)

If you understand this, then you are amongst those whom Allah have illuminated their hearts, but if you do not, then you have to start from *Alif*.

The Holy Prophet ﷺ has said, "Blessed once is the one who saw me and believed in me and blessed seven times is the one who did not see me and believed in me" (*Musnad Ahmad*).

بسم الله الرحمن الرحيم

Question 15 – Subud

What is Subud?

Bismillah and salutations upon *Rasul Allah* ﷺ, the Seal and the completion of the cycle of Prophethood and Messagehood. He brought the complete teaching to all of creations until time enters eternity. He brought the Holy Qur'an, the methodology, and the spiritual cosmology. The Holy Qur'an is complete in its Revelation, but the unfolding of its meanings to humanity will never end. This is the true way to travel back to the Source of Love, Knowledge, and Illumination.

Since the time of the Holy Prophet ﷺ, many strange men and women have come and gone and when they died, their teachings died with them. However, because of the modern technology of the last century, many new ways to electronically record audio and video were discovered and, as a result, many of these 'teachings' continue. This is not because they have any spiritual value, but because it is now possible to retain them indefinitely. We supplicate our Beloved Allah to protect us from such people that fill the internet and the like with misguidance in the guise of "spirituality." It is a very dangerous time and we have to be extremely vigilant in order to protect that which matters most – our soul and our spiritual well-being.

As for the founder of Subud, Mr. Muhammad Subuh, the only positive legacy he has left behind him is that many of his followers, which numbered around 10,000 at the time, have embraced Islam. As for the rest of his teaching, there is nothing in it worth mentioning or contemplating upon. He had nothing to offer but confusing practices with a very dangerous Javanese tradition thrown in of opening oneself to other forces, demonic in nature, which have the capability to become lethal or cause very serious mental illnesses. Below are a few short lines about this man and his teaching:

Bapak Muhammad Subuh Sumohadiwidjojo was born 1901 in Java, Indonesia, and died in 1987. As a young man he claimed to have received a series of intense experiences that he believed gave him contact with a spiritual energy from a higher power. By the 1930s, he believed that it was his task to transmit this energy - which he called *latihan kejiwaan* (Indonesian for "spiritual exercise") - to others, but that he was not to seek people out but simply to wait for those who asked for it!!

In 1956, Pak Subuh, or "Bapak" as he was called by members of Subud, was invited to England by J. G. Bennett (an ex-pupil of Gurdjieff), where many Westerners joined his organisation. He was then asked to go to other countries such as the United States and Australia. In this way, Subud spread rapidly around the world. When he died in 1987 he left many talks on audio tape, video, and in print, which Subud uses to guide the organisation he founded.

Muhammad Subuh wrote in his autobiography that, about the year 1932, he had a visionary visit to the highest heaven, the "Seventh Heaven." By his account, one night he felt drowsy and went to lie down in bed. Instead of falling asleep, he felt himself "lengthen, widen, and expand into a sphere" and then entered a great space. He saw a group of stars far away and was told that it was the universe he had left behind. He then travelled at great speed through a great expanse and beyond were "mountain-like cones of light, seven of them, one stacked upon another." He described how he entered the cones of light one after another until he entered the seventh, the last. Then he returned to earth and saw what looked like stars in the sky but later realised they were the lights of Semarang, the hometown where he lived. He even tarried a little over the rooftop of his own house trying to lift up some roof tiles with his fingers but instead found himself inside his own room. It was about the time of *Subuh* or dawn. In his description Muhammad Subuh implied the seventh cone of light represents the highest heaven. It is likely because of this description of his ascension that he insisted that his autobiography be published only after his death though it was completed much earlier.

Imagination and false vision are very dangerous tools. If not checked with the proper spiritual practices under an authentic teacher with the connection to the founder of *al-Isra wa al-Miraj* (The Night Journey and the Ascension), then it may bring disaster and damnation. If you wish to know more about the authentic teaching, you should read about the life of the Holy Prophet ﷺ and the lives of the great saints of Islam. And Allah speaks the truth and He guides to the Straight Path. *Wa ma tawfiq illa billah*. And there is no success except with Allah.

Question 16 – Departure of our Muqaddam

What does his departure mean for our Muqaddam?

Many brothers and sisters have asked me about the inevitable departure of our dear Muqaddam Sahib. Our Beloved Creator and Sustainer did not make it His business to give us the time of our arrival and the time of our departure. However, for a chosen few people of our Beloved Allah, this divine secret could be given to them. The Holy Prophet ﷺ always told us to be prepared and this preparation is not something that you can complete in just one day. It takes years of effort through the Grace of the All-Gracious One. Death looks at every one of us five times a day. Are we destined to go at that look or are there more breaths written for us to take?

Allah told us in the Holy Qur'an:

يَٰٓأَيُّهَا ٱلنَّاسُ ٱتَّقُوا۟ رَبَّكُمُ ٱلَّذِى خَلَقَكُم مِّن نَّفْسٍ وَٰحِدَةٍ

وَخَلَقَ مِنْهَا زَوْجَهَا وَبَثَّ مِنْهُمَا رِجَالًا كَثِيرًا وَنِسَآءً

وَٱتَّقُوا۟ ٱللَّهَ ٱلَّذِى تَسَآءَلُونَ بِهِۦ وَٱلْأَرْحَامَ إِنَّ ٱللَّهَ كَانَ

عَلَيْكُمْ رَقِيبًا

O Mankind! Be conscious of your Sustainer, who has created you out of one living entity, and out of it created its mate, and out of the two spread abroad a multitude of men and women. And remain conscious of God, in whose name you demand (your rights) from one another and of these ties of kinship. Verily, Allah is ever-watchful over you.

(Holy Qur'an 4:1)

So, what is the condition of a man of the calibre of our Muqaddam Ahmad Salih McCauley? The man who we loved very, very much. We do miss him terribly, but we do not argue with Allah's decree. We say what the Holy One gave us to say, these most beautiful, illuminating words:

إِنَّا لِلَّهِ وَإِنَّآ إِلَيْهِ رَٰجِعُونَ

From Allah we come and to Allah we return

(Holy Qur'an 2:156)

One of our great Saints and learned Masters, Shah Waliallah of Delhi, put it together for us in a way that we can understand the stages that one goes through after we go through in his article "The Nature of the Soul."[4] May the Beloved Allah reward our Shaykh for everything he enlightened us with and may Allah shower limitless blessing upon all of them and as the Holy Prophet ﷺ supplicated, "You have gone ahead and, *insha'Allah,* we are following close behind."

[4] *The Treasure* Issue 34, page 2, Almiraj Sufi & Islamic Study Centre.

Question 17 – Belief and Action

What is belief and actions?

ٱللَّهَ حَبَّبَ إِلَيْكُمُ ٱلْإِيمَٰنَ وَزَيَّنَهُۥ فِى قُلُوبِكُمْ

Allah has endeared the Faith to you, and has made it beautiful in your hearts

(Holy Qur'an 49:7)

The Holy Prophet Muhammad ﷺ said, "I leave you two things. As long as you follow these you will never go astray: Allah's Book and the Sunnah of the Prophet" (*Muwatta*).

The Holy Prophet ﷺ also said, "Belief is in the heart and the actions of the limbs confirm or deny it."

When you leave this earthly realm, the only transportation you have is what you bring with you (in the form of your belief and actions). On that day, some people will be overwhelmed and will collapse and not be able to move any further. Then the Salutations of the Holy Prophet ﷺ that they performed will come and lift them up and carry him on to a state of bliss. Another one will collapse and the light of his ablution will come and pick him up and carry him onwards. For another who collapses, his *salah* (prayers) will come and assist him. For another, his *dhikr* of *la ilaha il Allah* will be his salvation. Even for the one who thinks he has nothing this testimony of faith is there to his credit. This word of testimony (*kalimah*) is so powerful that it could outweigh any negative actions that were committed during the lifetime of the person, especially with a strong belief in the Oneness of Allah and the Message of the Holy Prophet Muhammad ﷺ.

The Holy Prophet ﷺ said, "Allah will save a man of his community the record of whose sins fills 99 books, each book extending as far as the eye can see. Against all this will be weighed the one good deed that he has, which is his witnessing that there is no god but Allah and that Muhammad is His Messenger, and it will outweigh all the rest" (*Musnad Ahmad, Jami' al-Tirmidhi, Mustadark al-Hakim,* and *Sunan Bayhaqi*).

Actions have a spirit and they could become a source of bliss when performed correctly. Allah says in the Holy Qur'an *wajtanibu* (Shun, eschew).

وَلَقَدْ بَعَثْنَا فِى كُلِّ أُمَّةٍ رَّسُولًا أَنِ ٱعْبُدُوا۟ ٱللَّهَ وَٱجْتَنِبُوا۟ ٱلطَّـٰغُوتَ

And indeed, within every community have We raised up a Messenger [entrusted with this message]: Worship God, and shun the powers of evil!

(Holy Qur'an 16:36)

Translated into English, it would say "don't do this" or "stay away from this." If you look a little deeper into this verse and what it means you will find that in Arabic the side of your body is called *janb*. *Sahib janb* is the one who is at your side. As they say, "I'm on your side." Here, Allah wants us to be on the side of the Qur'an, on His side. So there are places where He says *wajtanibu* "don't do this" and other verses where He says "Do this." One is a positive action and the other is a negative action and each one has a different illumination. So, if you take the Qur'an on one side and on the other side you have the Sunnah of the Holy Prophet ﷺ, then you are covered and completely protected on both sides.

It's amazing how people can doubt. With today's technologies everything is transmitted immediately, and information and knowledge is abundant. The transmission comes through the walls and the ceiling, straight to your smart phone. There is something ready to pull the energy in – you don't see it, but it's there and you take it on belief. It's the same with the People of Allah, they could be sitting anywhere, in a closed room, and one could project himself and see a long distance. That essence inside one's self becomes so powerful when it is not busy with other diversions within the self. When everything is tuned properly and is working properly, then when you focus on something, your message gets there.

For the one who believes, no proof is necessary, but for the one who disbelieves, no amount of proof will suffice. And Allah speaks the Truth and He guides to the straight path.

بسم الله الرحمن الرحيم

Question 18 – Sufism

What is Sufism?

Sufism (*tasawwuf*) is the esoteric teaching of Islam. We are living in the 21st Century, the age of instant communication, so we would hope by now that Sufism does not require extensive explanation. This teaching has been made more accessible around the world not only by way of the internet, but by the thousands of books written on the subject and the biographies of the great Saints of Islam. We are not surprised when we discovered that the best-selling books around the world are by the great Sufi mystical poets such as Rumi and Hafiz. For the sake of clarification and explanation, we put forward a short introduction to this great esoteric, heart teaching of Islam. Everything has an inward and an outward aspect, and Islam is no exception.

There are many different explanations of where the name "*Sufi*" began. One is *suf* - the Arabic word meaning "wool."

It has been said in the Traditions of the Holy Prophet ﷺ that the Prophet Musa (Moses) عَلَيْهِ السَّلَامُ was wearing wool when he went to speak with God on Mount Sinai. In the early days wool was inexpensive and rough, worn by ascetics as a sign of humility and detachment. Wool is the opposite of silk, which represents wealth and material comforts. In some traditions the Sufis are connected with the Companions of the Holy Prophet ﷺ. There was a group of very highly devoted and sincere seekers of God named *Ahl al-Suffa,* the People of the Bench. They spent their lives in a state of remembrance of God and complete detachment from this world.

It has also been said that Sufism is related to the root of the word *safa* - to purify - here meaning to purify the heart of everything other than God. There are many names attached to this teaching. The Sufis nonetheless say, "If one says he is a Sufi, he is not a Sufi." To be a Sufi is to be in a state of complete awareness of the self, in service to the creations, and complete awareness of the Divine Supreme Being (Allah).

Between the Supreme Being and us there are no veils, but between us and Allah there are 70,000 veils of darkness and light. The goal of self-transformation is to remove all the veils between us and God. The final veil is the "I," the sense of separateness we each carry. To remove this is far from easy. Ask yourself "How can I take the 'I' out of me?"

The Sufis take as their starting point the Unity of God - *la ilaha il Allah* - There is no god but One God; There is no reality but One Reality. It is not that we have to acknowledge the Unity of God. God does not need our confirmation. It is for our own benefit that we make this declaration. When one starts with Unity it is easy to integrate all the different "I's" which have no function except to confuse and mislead us. For this reason, the Sufis use the remembrance of Allah (*dhikr*) in all of its forms, including prayer, meditation, fasting, charity and selfless actions in order to awaken the subtle centres of the self.

In Islam, and therefore Sufism, there are seven states of consciousness that have been mentioned in the Holy Qur'an. When we progress through them we will reach the

Ultimate Truth and the Ultimate Unity of Realisation of God. It is hard and, at the same time, it is easy. If we are sincere and if we desire and really wish to be with God, then, as Allah says in the Holy Qur'an:

وَنَحْنُ أَقْرَبُ إِلَيْهِ مِنْ حَبْلِ ٱلْوَرِيدِ

and We are closer to him than his jugular vein

(Holy Qur'an 50:16)

And in a *Hadith Qudsi*, "If you take one step towards Me, I will come running towards you."

So, the first step on the journey is, as we mentioned, the acknowledgment of God, which includes the acceptance of 124,000 prophets and messengers of God who have been sent to humanity and to the entire creation at large. This should not be difficult since we did not create ourselves, but were created by the Merciful and Loving Allah, who is the Creator and Sustainer of all things.

The last Prophet and Messenger of God is the Holy Prophet Muhammad ﷺ. If we acknowledge this, then the second step is to worship, because there is no point in acknowledging God if we do not obey Him. As a Sufi poet said, "You disobey Allah, and you claim His Love. That is indeed a very strange kind of love!" If you are truly a lover of God, you will obey Him because the lover is in a state of total surrender to his Beloved. So, worship you must! However, worship is not just the movements of the body. It is a state of knowledge, because in the true sense you cannot worship something that you do not know. So, the Sufis say "Worship!" Worship in the Arabic tradition is called *'ibadah*. *'Ibadah* should take us to *'ubudiyya,* meaning slavehood. If worship does not produce this result, then it has not been done properly. The highest state of consciousness is to be completely and totally submitted to our Beloved, Allah.

There are four stages of practice and understanding as taught by the Holy Prophet ﷺ:

Shari'ah (religious law)
Tariqa (the mystical path)
Haqiqah (Truth)
Ma'rifa (Gnosis)

Each stage is built upon the ones that go before.

There are also other steps to take in this method of development of the self. It is highly recommended to observe the month of fasting every year (the Holy month of Ramadan) in order to experience something of hunger and to tame and control the animal-self. The Murshid, or teacher, of a Sufi order or school to whom one attaches oneself, may recommend other fasts if they are required.

There is also *zakat,* the poor tax, which deals with material wealth. When we practise *zakat,* which requires 2.5% of our wealth to be given to the needy, then, according to the esoteric teaching, we are learning detachment, generosity, and many other qualities. We must know that the best gift one can give to others is a heart full of love and respect for all the creations of God. The required poor tax is the absolute minimum. It is much better to be generous at all times in every area of life. This practice will accelerate the illumination of the self.

Additionally, there is the *Hajj,* or pilgrimage. The Holy Prophet ﷺ said, "Whoever dies without the intention to go on the Pilgrimage may die on a different faith than that of surrender to Allah." One must strive to perform pilgrimage to the House of Allah once in a lifetime. However, the real pilgrimage is to travel to one's heart because it is the Real House of Allah. Allah says in a *Hadith Qudsi,* "Neither My heavens nor My earth contain Me, but the heart of My believing slave contains Me."

Die Before You Die

The Sufis use all of these methods, and more, to transform the self. It is common knowledge that the ego-self cannot surrender to itself. From day one we are learning from our parents, our peers, schoolteachers, our university lecturers, and the masters of whatever trade we undertake. There is always someone at the beginning who must show us how to learn. No one is born knowing everything and the Sufi aspirant is no exception. In *tasawwuf* there is something called the Spiritual Genealogy. In some parts of the world it is called *mukaffaf* - people of the hand. That is, you must take the hand of the one nearest to you to link you to the chain which goes back to the first teacher who brought this teaching to us, the Holy Prophet Muhammad ﷺ, who links us to Allah Himself. It is like a magnetic circle. The one who attaches himself becomes like a magnet, receiving the spiritual blessings (*baraka*) and participating in the Universal Remembrance of God, because this teaching is for all humanity. It is Universal, it is fresh and unadulterated, and it gives you access to everything that your heart desires and everything that you wish for on this earth and beyond.

Almiraj Sufi & Islamic Study Centre was established in Australia in 1983. It provides all those who want to know - and who really want to know - with a large range of books on the Sufi traditions and their original sources as well other traditions. So, I hope this introduction helps to give you some idea, but if you want more than the menu - the kitchen and the cook are available. May your search bring you success in this life and the next.

And may Allah fill our hearts and yours with Peace, Love, and Knowledge and Guide us all to Him, by Him. And there is no success except by Allah. Ameen

Question 19 – The Beginning

How do I Begin?

Regarding their awareness of what is to come and the beginning of the new cycle, humanity can be divided into three groups. The first group, of which not much need be said, are the ones who are oblivious to the impending disaster.

The second group are those who worry about the end of the cycle. Of this group we can say that they are already partly conscious or you could say that they have accumulated enough awareness to see the shortcomings of humanity. In this regard they are saved and yet not saved. They are like the passengers in a bus that is racing downhill without brakes. The fact that they can see that there are no brakes will not stop the bus in its destructive progress into the abyss. They can prepare themselves for the end of the road but they are unable to change the direction or halt the movement of the vehicle. The knowledge that events are spinning out of control can lead to states of anxiety, disillusionment, and negative thoughts, which, in turn, can contribute to the behaviour of the ones who have caused this catastrophe. The saving grace of this second group is that they saw the wrongdoing and that they are still able to see it. Their downfall lies in their total belief in material things and humanism and they are, thereby, unable to change the cycle of destruction.

There is a saying of the Holy Prophet Muhammad ﷺ that prayer and supplication can change the course of destiny. If we want to be amongst those to change the course of our own and our collective destiny, we must take action. We cannot seek to change things by wishing to change the various causes. We have to go right back to the primary cause and connect ourselves to the source of life itself, which is Allah. We become part of the third group by acknowledging this fact and working on ourselves to change the darkness within us to light, change our negativity to positive thought, speech, and action. This is done by following the way of the great and final Messenger of God, Muhammad ﷺ. He saw the future of humanity, or you could say that he came from the future itself, because of his miraculous powers from the Absolute and his realisation in God. He is the Most Beloved of God and is the one who said, “Creation is the family of God.” And “The most beloved of God are those who care for the family of God.” We truly believe with no doubt whatsoever that if we follow in his footsteps and practice the method he brought to us all, then the course of humanity will change for the better. If we want to live our lives like a Hollywood movie, then we can sit back in our comfortable chairs and wait for the end. Most surely, the end will come. To live in darkness requires no effort.

From the treasures of the teaching of our Holy Prophet Muhammad ﷺ we are presenting the following formulas for the sake of Light, so that Light may fill our hearts, our thoughts, our speech, and actions. Then, through the power of the Love of God in our prayer, supplication, and meditations, we will be able, with God's permission, to change the course of humanity so that peace may fill our lives.

The spiritual practice known as *al-asaas* (the foundation of human consciousness) is overflowing with spiritual blessing (*baraka*) and, with the Grace of Allah, this spiritual energy will bring benefit to any genuine and sincere seeker of truth who turns to this exalted method of remembrance with need and humility.

In preparation, one should make ablutions with clean, flowing water (*wudhu*). Then isolate yourself in a quiet room or corner and be seated comfortably. Recite, with awareness and purpose, the five formulas, or as much as you can. On completion make supplication to God, and with His help, one will be able to change oneself and to help humanity and all the creations of God.

This practice is to be completed twice each day. The best times for the performance of this blessed exercise is in the early morning a short while before sunrise, and in the late afternoon just before sunset. The recitation of the afternoon may be made after sunset if circumstances require it.

al-Asaas (The Foundation)

بِسْمِ ٱللَّهِ ٱلرَّحْمَـٰنِ ٱلرَّحِيمِ

Bismillahi Rahmaan-ir Raheem (Repeat 100 times)

In the Name of Allah, the Compassionate, the Merciful

أَسْتَغْفِرُ ٱللَّهَ ٱلْعَظِيمَ هُوَ ٱلتَّوَّابُ ٱلرَّحِيمُ

Astaghfirullah al-'Adheem, Huwa-t-Tawaabu Raheem

(Repeat 100 times)

I seek the forgiveness of Allah Almighty, He is the Oft-Returning, the Merciful

لَا إِلَٰهَ إِلَّا ٱللَّهُ

Laa ilaha il Allah (Repeat 100 times)

There is no god but Allah

يَا دَايِمُ

Yaa Da'yem (Repeat 300 times)

O Everlasting One!

ٱللَّهُمَّ صَلِّ عَلَىٰ سَيِّدِنَا مُحَمَّدٍ وَآلِهِ وَسَلِّمْ

Allahumma salli 'ala Sayyidina Muhammadin wa aalihi wa sallam (Repeat 100 times)

O Allah! Send salutations upon our Master Muhammad and his family and give them Peace

These spiritual formulas are a gift from God to humanity and contain an abundance of secrets. Each recitation can generate so much spiritual energy in one's system that one's supplications will have wings to fly to God.

Wa ma taufi'iq illa billah. And there is no success except by Allah.

Question 20 – Disentanglement

With all of the difficulties and troubles that I have, is it really possible to smooth out my life and disentangle myself from all of this?

The path of *tasawwuf* is also known as the path of disentanglement. We are all born into this life in a pure state, straight from the Essence of Allah. In the Sufi teaching there are three main development stages of the human - from 0-7 years of age, from 7-14 years of age and from 14-21 years of age. From the time we are born up until around the 7 year mark, our parents are responsible for guiding us to right actions and moulding us in the proper way of behaviour. When we reach the age of around 7 or before, the conscience should have developed and we become aware of right and wrong and begin to be responsible for our own actions. As we grow and develop further, what we call grafting or conditioning takes place. This comes not only from parents, but teachers, society, peer groups, and, later, from further education and the working environment.

Each action that we perform will leave its mark on us. If we make good actions, then our hearts become purified. If the actions that we perform are of the negative type, then what we call "rust" will accumulate on the heart as black spots, which eventually can blot out the light of God which is present in all of us. If the person does not turn away from their negative activities, it is possible for the heart to become sealed and the conscience may die altogether. Someone like this would be in the stage of *nafs al-ammarratan bi su'*, the self prone to evil or the criminal self.

The fact that you have asked the question is in itself an indication that your conscience is at least partially awake and this is a good thing. There are many tools that are used within the teaching to purify the self and increase us in knowledge and light. The Holy Prophet ﷺ said the hearts rust just like iron rusts and the polish for the heart is the Remembrance of Allah.

In the beginning of our travel, we may have certain debts to pay, whether they be towards our own self or to others. We are trying to move forward, but there are certain things within the self which are resistant to change and certain things that are attached to us like hooks that try to drag us back. It's like having an elastic band tied around your waist. So, you go, go, go, go, go and you think you've made it, but then you get pulled back again. It is important to make sure that every step we take is on the path of Allah, that we correct our actions and do what is required from us by Allah, Most High.

As you progress, you will find that the further you move away from your past life and increase your knowledge and practices, the more and more stretched the attachment will become and eventually it will just snap. Like an elastic band, the force of the breakage can also propel you much faster along the Path, like a temporary turbo-charge, giving you a feeling of lightness and freedom.

It is most definitely possible to disentangle yourself from your old actions and way of life, neutralise all of that, and live a pure, clean, and peaceful life. It does take a little bit of elbow grease, though. You will need to roll up your sleeves and put some effort into the work.

Question 21 – Initiation (*Bay'ah*)

What is the Rite of *Bay'ah*, or Initiation, and is it Really Necessary?

Usually, it is only the people who are connected to *tasawwuf* or the ones who are travelling along the path that will enquire about the *bay'ah*.

It is the purpose of all religions to take their adherents back to the Source, which is God. We will not delve into other spiritual paths but concentrate here on the final teaching of Allah to humanity, which is Islam. In reality, as human beings, there are several pledges or covenants that we make in our spiritual lives.

A young man asked me once if it was possible to become a Sufi without making the *shahadah*. It is impossible to develop your awareness and to learn how to unite yourself without this declaration. The business of the Murshid is to make sure that the travellers under his care become aware of the first covenant, the first *bay'ah* that they took in the world of the spirit. This first covenant was when Allah asked all of the spirits *Alastu Bi Rubbikum*? "Am I not your Lord?" and all of us answered "Yes." This occurred in the realm of the spirit, before our descent to this realm, when we were still in the "mind" of Allah. We were not separate and did not have any identity as we were still in a state of essence. This is the first thing that the traveller must know. You have taken a covenant with Allah, even though you may not be aware of it.

It is an absolutely necessary step to make the declaration of faith, even for those who were born into a Muslim family. It is required from every person once in his lifetime. When the Shaytan was tempting the Holy Prophet Jesus عليه السلام, he said, "Say *la ilaha il Allah.*" Jesus عليه السلام responded to him saying, "I will say it, but not on your authority." If he عليه السلام had, then the Shaytan would have become his teacher and misled him because, and, by that action, he would have been accepting a transmission of consciousness from him.

In *tasawwuf* there is something called *talqin* (to teach or instruct), meaning that the Shaykh or Murshid says something and you repeat after him. There is a transmission of spiritual energy (*baraka*) that is contained in those words. When the Holy Prophet ﷺ was teaching his cousin Ali رضي الله عنه, the first child to enter Islam, he summoned him to his presence and they sat knees together, facing each other. The Holy Prophet ﷺ spoke, saying the *Shahadah* three times "*Ashadu an la ilaha il Allah*" and Ali رضي الله عنه listened and then Ali رضي الله عنه repeated it while the Holy Prophet ﷺ closed his eyes and listened. This is known in the Holy Qur'an as the *kalimat al-tayyibah* (the Good Word or the Good Tree). It is firmly rooted in the ground and its branches reach towards the heavens (see Holy Qur'an 14:24). When you, as a human being, have realisation of the knowledge of this word (*kalima*) and it becomes part of you, then you become like the tree, firmly rooted in the ground as a slave of Allah, but your realisation is beyond the heavens itself.

In the presence of Allah, there is a column of light which, when the slave of Allah makes *dhikr* of this particular phrase - *la ilaha il Allah,* repeating it many times over, this column vibrates and attracts the attention of the Divine. Allah says:

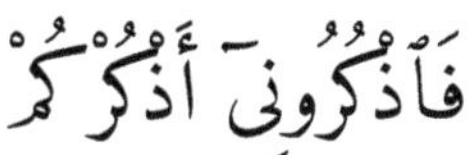

Remember Me, and I shall remember you
(Holy Qur'an 2:152)

This is the first step - the *shahadah,* the declaration of faith. If you say it with real certainty and consciousness (*yaqin*) it will be strong enough to take you back to your original state of consciousness and you will hear the echo of "Am I not your Lord?"

The process of the inner teachings of *tasawwuf* is to take us back to that state, which is not absent from us, but it is veiled from us. Because of the environment that we live in - this world - we become veiled and enter a state of forgetfulness. So many verses in the Holy Qur'an are there to remind us of our origin and wake us up to our original state of purity.

Now, here we are on this earth in our state of forgetfulness. So, Allah sent 124,000 Holy Prophets and Messengers to remind us, the Holy Prophet Muhammad ﷺ being the final Prophet and Messenger to humanity.

Allah said that whoever pledges allegiance to his Prophet, he gives his allegiance to Allah, the hand of Allah is above their hands.[5] This verse of the Holy Qur'an forms the basis of the Pledge of Allegiance (*bay'ah*) which is recited by the Shaykh or Murshid when he accepts someone as a *murid* and is modelled on the pledge that the Companions of the Holy Prophet ﷺ made at the Tree of Hudaibiyah.

If a person develops a certain potential he may begin to realise that there is more to this *deen* (lit. life transaction) than just the outer shell. The outer shell is only there to protect what is inside. As a person develops, they begin to notice different verses of the Holy Qur'an that deal with

---

[5] "Behold, all who pledge their allegiance to you (Muhammad) pledge their allegiance to Allah: the hand of Allah is over their hands. Hence, he who breaks his oath, breaks it only to his own hurt; whereas he who remains true to what he has pledged unto Allah, on him will He bestow a reward supreme" (Holy Qur'an 48:10).

the higher consciousness and with contemplation. To travel further is an individual struggle. This is a voluntary action in order to bring you closer to the love of Allah and bring you to a state of *wilaya* (friendship or sainthood).

The first initiation from above and the first initiation from below are very, very important. To go forward towards the spiritual initiation, to give allegiance to one who is able to take you towards Allah, is a very great blessing. If one is fortunate enough, eager enough, determined enough, and lucky enough, this can happen.

This pledge of allegiance is given to the *nawab*, the representative or deputy of the Holy Prophet Muhammad ﷺ. The Holy Prophet ﷺ said, "The people of knowledge among my followers are like the prophets of the tribe of Israel." There is a chain of transmission (*silsilat*), which has always been there, from the time of the Holy Prophet ﷺ down to us here in the present day. Connecting yourself to this chain is how you enter this process of initiation and realisations which will take you back to your original state of consciousness in the presence of your Lord and allow you to experience once again the celestial sound of *Alastu Bi Rubbikum*? – "Am I not your Lord?"

When one finds a Sufi Order and becomes initiated, then this forms the second confirmed initiation. The secret of what is contained in that moment between Murshid and murid is so very powerful. It can lead you on to the third initiation, which connects directly with the presence of the Holy Prophet Muhammad ﷺ. This is a confirmation of the first initiation - bearing witness with the eye of reality (*'ayn al-yaqin*) that Muhammad is the Messenger of Allah ﷺ.

Question 22 – Initiation (*Bay'ah*) at a Distance

Can I take *Bay'ah* (Allegiance) Long Distance? And do I need my husband's permission to take *bay'ah*?

Within this great teaching, everything is based on *adab* (proper manners). Like anything in life, when we want to learn something, we get registered in the course and begin to learn. The highest thing that any human being could endeavour to learn is the spiritual teaching of Islam (*tasawwuf*). It deals directly with our success in this life and in the next. The concept of *bay'ah* is not new in Islam. The Holy Prophet ﷺ used to take *bay'ah* from his companions, both male and female. The most famous example of this is *Bay'ah al-Ridhwan* at Hudaibiyah.

When the Holy Prophet ﷺ wanted to perform the Hajj, but was prevented from doing so by the people of Mecca, the negotiation took place and Sayyidina 'Uthman bin 'Affan رضي الله عنه, the third successor of the Holy Prophet ﷺ, was sent to negotiate with the people of

Mecca. He was gone for some time when a rumour circulated that they had killed him.

The Holy Prophet ﷺ took *bay'ah* from those who were present at that place and then he took his right hand and placed it in his left hand and said, "This is the hand of 'Uthman" and completed the *bay'ah* for him in his absence. This has become known as *bay'ah 'uthmaniyyah*. When a *murid* is physically far away from the Shaykh, it is possible to take *bay'ah 'uthmaniyyah* and it is valid – in order to connect oneself to the Shaykh's genealogy of teachers, right back to the Holy Prophet ﷺ, and receive the *baraka* and the teaching. In our time, that could be implemented by writing, a phone call or other means of communication.

There are many other forms of *bay'ah* as well. There is the *bay'ah* of *tabarruk*, to receive the spiritual blessings (*baraka*) of being connected to the *tariqa*, but you do not necessarily travel the course of the teaching. In our time, many people who think they are Sufis have taken such a *bay'ah*. If a woman wishes to study under the guidance of a Murshid/Shaykh and if her husband cannot provide her with the spiritual teaching, then it is her duty to do so – with his permission or without. That should suffice to fulfil one's duty to the *deen* of Allah and the Messenger ﷺ. This should bring peace, *baraka*, tranquillity, belonging, and fulfilment of the advice of the holiest human being to walk this earth, the final Prophet and Messenger to the creations ﷺ. And endless salutations and peace be upon him in every blink of an eye and in every breath that is taken. May the Merciful and Loving Allah guide you and protect you.

Question 23 – Seeking God

People all seem to be searching for something, even though they voice it differently. Is there one thing that *everyone* is looking for?

Concerning this, Shaykh Jalaluddin Rumi ﵀ relates a story in his Mathnawi:

Once upon a time a man gave a Persian, an Arab, a Turk and a Greek, whom he saw together, some money. In doing them this kindness, he said, "Buy whatever you like with this money."

One of the four, the Persian, said, "Let's buy some 'angür' with it."

The Arab disagreed. "Don't be stupid! I don't want any 'angür'. I want some 'inab'."

The third person, the Turk, didn't like either of those ideas. "I don't want any 'angür' or 'inab'. Let's buy some 'üzüm'," he said.

The Greek, who had been watching what was going on, cried, "Stop this foolishness. I want some 'istafil'. Let's buy some 'istafil' with this money!"

All at once, the four of them started arguing, each man yelling that they should buy what he wanted. Fists flew and there was a big fight. Before long a scholar, who was passing by, broke up the fight and asked what the problem was.

The Persian said, "I want to buy some 'angür' with the money that was given."

"No, we're going to buy some 'inab'," protested the Arab.

"I say, let's buy some 'üzüm'," shouted the Turk.

"We're going to buy some 'istafil' with our money," insisted the Greek.

The scholar understood that these four people speaking in different languages actually all wanted the same thing. He said, "Be quiet and listen to me. I'm going to buy what all of you want with this money. Believe me!" Then he went and bought some grapes, which is what each of them was trying to express in his own way.

Allah is within you

We always seem to be looking outside of our own selves when we look for Allah, when in reality the whole program is internal. The Holy Prophet Jesus عليه السلام said, "The kingdom of Allah is within you." Allah says in a Holy Saying, "Neither My heavens nor My earth can contain Me, but the heart of My believing slave contains Me." The (spiritual) human heart – that is where Allah is to be found.

We said earlier that when we bear witness "there is no god but One God and Muhammad is the Messenger of God" - this statement is only required from a person once in their lifetime. But the realisation of *la ilaha il Allah,* "There is no god but One God," this must be worked on throughout our life. Every day in our life we must remember this, we must bring it to realisation. The more we have realisation of this phrase, the more tranquil and peaceful we become.

If we think the world owes us something, that certain things must be given to us, or that we have rights over this or that – this is called lack of *adab* with Allah. This means that you have a lack of etiquette with Allah. Allah wants us to understand that He is the Owner of all things and that He is the Master of all things. Remember that this is for our own benefit as Allah does not need us to acknowledge anything about His Sovereignty.

When you realise that something is not yours, you don't worry too much about parting with it, and when you think about it, it is as Imam al-Ghazali said, "this life is like travelling on a boat." The boat stops at a beautiful island and some of the passengers disembark and walk about. They find many wonderful things there: jewels, fruits, and all kinds of magical things. Some of them look at the island and say, "there are many wonderful things here, but this is not my place." So, they take what is necessary and return to the boat. Some of the people thought it was very nice on the island, decided to stay, and began making plans to build their houses and settle there. The ones who came first got a better place on the island, but when darkness came all the other wonderful things there came out from their places as well. Tigers, snakes, and many other predators came out and destroyed all who stayed behind.

It is the same in the spiritual journey.

This life is like sitting in someone's house as a guest. The host passes a beautiful tray to the guests full of beautiful things for them to see. He says to them, "you may each take something as a souvenir," so each guest in turn chooses something and passes the tray to the next guest. Until it reaches one person who grabs on and doesn't want to let go of it. He says, "this is mine," and he is told, "no, this is not yours, it is meant to move around." The host recommends that we look at it, don't damage anything, handle it with care, take what you need, but you cannot keep hold onto it. This is the problem with this life – we take it, we want to keep it, we want to store it, we damage it, and treat it with disrespect. When it comes time for someone to take it from us, we go screaming and kicking.

People can become earth-bound and cause themselves and others many difficulties. There is a great difference between the one who wants to leave this life for the meeting with their Lord and the one who is earth-bound. For the one who wants to hurry to the meeting, it is as if their coffin almost flies on its own to the burial place. But for the other, it is very heavy and drags down those trying to transport it. One is prepared and the other is not. Preparation is very necessary.

Question 24 – Realisation of the Names and Attributes

When we refer to "seeing" Allah, is that to see Essence, or is it the Attributes or the Names? It isn't possible to "see" Essence, is it?

The first experience that one could have when they "see" Allah is the experience of the Attributes; not the Names of Allah, but the Attributes. Accidently sometimes people could see one of the Names in the Attributes, but they wouldn't recognise it as such. Sometimes in a moment of seriousness in their life, if certain conditions are prevailing at that moment, then someone could "break through" and experience something of the Names. This is a glimpse of the Truth. Real experience begins to happen when someone could truly experience the Names of Allah. This happens when you embody a particular Name, or have realisation of that particular Name. For example, one of the Names of Allah is *al-'Aleem,* the Knower. If you were to practice with regards to that particular Name until you become the embodiment of that Name, then you would become *'alim,* a knower, and you would begin to have knowledge of many secret things.

Some of the practices within *tasawwuf* are specialised in this particular science - the science of the Names. Some people are not concerned so much with realisations in Allah, but they want to connect themselves solely to the functions of the Names of Allah. This is where you could find magic and witchcraft and power and such.

Someone may also go to a Sufi Master and learn how to become a healer, through the Name *al-Shafi,* the One who gives healing. He starts to practice and begins to learn some of the secrets from Allah regarding the functions of plants and trees and herbs. It is almost like there is a communication between him and the vegetable kingdom; so, he just knows what that certain thing's functions are.

Realisation in Allah, of course, is another story in the sense that there is Oneness with Allah. One could have an experience of Allah after unlocking certain things within his self, meaning that he overcomes the animal-self, not destroy it or kill it as some people may think, but gets it under control. It is interesting that, particularly in the West, you hear people say, "Allah speaks to me," "Allah told me," or "Allah told me that" - this is belittling Allah and makes it seem like He just sits on the switchboard waiting for their call. This is, of course, an illusion. Allah can be reached, but you have to use the proper mechanism and development. This cannot be done through the physical, or the psychic, or by way of the personality. Just because you may be charming and have a very nice personality, you may think Allah will speak to you. It does not work on that principle. You have to unlock the mechanism inside so that you may be slowly prepared to experience the power of Allah within us.

This is all connected to the heart. You could say that each subtle centre (*latifa*) has a way of opening a certain aspect of the heart. There is the heart, the spirit, the secret. When we speak of the secret, when this *latifa* begins to open, that is where a person starts to experience the Divine aspect of Allah. That is why they call it "secret," because this is when you begin to know what Divinity is about. This is your own secret, and you know it within your own self. It's like you now have knowledge of what is going on behind the curtains. At this point, you no longer operate on blind faith, but you go beyond belief to a state of perfection (*ihsan*), perfection; a state of witnessing that which you believe in. In the stage of the secret (*sirr*) sometimes it cannot be expressed in words, because at times it is beyond words and beyond forms. To bring it into words and forms could be quite difficult.

As far as your question about experiencing Essence, the experience of Essence is obliterating. If one experiences it, this is absolute annihilation in the Essence of Allah and he would not be conscious of the experience because it is beyond consciousness. The Prophet Moses عليه السلام asked, "O my Lord! Show (Yourself) to me, that I may gaze upon Your countenance." Allah said, "'By no means can you see Me (direct); But look upon the mount; if it abides in its place, then shall you see Me'. When his Lord manifested His glory on the Mount, He made it as dust. And Moses fell down in a swoon" (Holy Qur'an 7:143). So, when

Allah unveiled just a tiny amount of His majesty, both Moses عَلَيْهِ السَّلَامُ and the mountain were obliterated.

There are many steps to take along the Path: travelling to Allah, travelling with Allah, travelling in Allah, and then, when you emerge, you are travelling by Allah. Between travelling in Allah and travelling *by* Allah, there are two major experiences, what we call in Arabic, *fana'* and *baqa'*; annihilation and abiding.

Many times you find that when you read the names of the Sufi Masters, you may find *al-faani fillah* or *al-baaqi billah*. These are titles for some of the Masters – "The one annihilated in Allah" or "The one abiding in Allah." So, the one "abiding in Allah" is in a state of ultimate nearness to Allah, without being Divine. This is all very interesting and it is important to have the information but don't allow yourself to live in a grand illusion. These things we are talking about here are very high states of consciousness and they require proper preparations. One should not misguide himself or be under the illusion that you have reached.

For a start, we have to know about our bodies and what they require from us in relation to the absolute teaching. How to utilise the body, how to utilise the personality, how to utilise the psyche, and how to properly utilise the spiritual teaching. Discipline has to be obtained. Once this is achieved, then the door to the King is never closed. To the one who said, "If you knock, Allah will open to you," Rabia al-Adawiyya replied, "Since when did He close His door?" His door is always open. It is mentioned in the Holy Qur'an that the doors of bliss are always open. The doors of separation, the doors of hell, they are shut - you have to knock on them and break into them to get in. The doors of mercy, the doors of knowledge, the doors of love, they are never shut. In order to attain a state of bliss is relatively easy, but to go to hell, you really have to work at it.

Freeing the Prisoner

The Holy Prophet ﷺ said, "The Lord descends every night to the lowest heaven when one-third of the night remains and says, 'Who will call upon Me, that I may answer Him? Who will ask of Me, that I may give him? Who will seek My forgiveness, that I may forgive him?'" The last portion of the night is when the body has less control over the spirit and it is much easier at that time to free it. It is said that the spirit is like a prisoner in the body with five guards, always there, keeping watch. The prison is the body and the five guards are the senses. When the guards are asleep, she sneaks out, wandering around, visiting home. But, as soon as one of the guards stirs, very quickly, she's back in again. You may be in the middle of a beautiful dream when you hear a noise or a mosquito bites you and smack, suddenly you are back in the body.

When you perform remembrance of Allah (*dhikr*) the body may start to sway gently with the activity of the spirit. At first, when you recite the *dhikr*, you just sit there quietly, like a mountain. The spirit is like a bird inside a cage, it begins to rock the cage and, sometimes, it can break free and fly.

This is the wonderful thing about the *dhikr* of Allah, it can make you fly. I have seen people in the gatherings of the Remembrance of Allah physically levitate. Not because they are doing it intentionally, they don't even realise that they are 1 or 2 metres in the air and someone next to them has to pull them back down again. These people have spiritualised their bodies to such an extent that the power of the spirit is stronger than the body. The whole work is to bring about that sensitivity and spiritualise the body so that it transforms from being a gross, solid mass, to becoming more fluid, to the point where it becomes like a cloud and can move about. So, the secret to the question that was asked is in the remembrance of Allah. For He says, "Remember Me and I will remember you." This remembering can come in the smallest things. Even an undesirable action that you have not committed because of your awareness that the eyes of Allah may be upon you – this can become a source of enlightenment.

Allah Loves the Sincere Supplicant

A man came to the great Sufi Master Junayd رحمه الله and asked him to make a prayer for him to become enlightened. So the Shaykh sat him down in front of him and made *dua'* for him. Instantly the man was transformed by a great surge and even Junayd رحمه الله was surprised. He made supplication to Allah in order to understand what had just happened. He رحمه الله said, "I've been talking with you for 25 years now and yet this man received enlightenment instantly. Am I doing something wrong?" The message came back to him, "No, no, We have you there because We love to hear you talking to Us. We do not want you to go away." But for the one who came and began whining about enlightenment, Allah said, "here, take it, and go away."

Allah enjoys listening to sincere supplications from His slaves. There is a story of the Prophet Moses عليه السلام and how when he was travelling, he came upon a shepherd boy who was sitting there, looking up to the sky, and saying, "Oh, Allah, I want to wash Your feet and comb Your beard and wash Your clothes for You" and saying all manner of things. Moses عليه السلام was terrified and shouted at the boy, "You there, be quiet, how could you speak like this? Allah doesn't have feet, or a beard, or clothing." His explanation of the Majesty of Allah left the boy in such a terrified state he could not look to the sky anymore. The Prophet Moses عليه السلام, who was the one who spoke to Allah, received a direct reprimand from the Almighty, "What did you do to my friend? You chased him away and scared him so much he can't talk to Me anymore." So, you see, Allah was happy to hear from him in his simplicity and sincerity of devotion - his innocent way of talking to Allah. It is not a condition that a person gets something quickly or not quickly, this is up to Allah. Maybe He just likes to hear us talk to Him. If you look at humanity today, how many people are praying around the globe and saying things like "change the condition of humanity," "give them more food," "give them more of this or that," "remove sickness," or "give people a decent life"? So many people are praying for these things, for the betterment of humanity. Allah does not just grant every request - imagine how many people pray for things that are at the opposite end of the scale? It would be chaos if every supplication was granted just like that.

Proximity Brings Understanding

Allah does not work according to *our* desires, He has His own program and plan for things. Our problem is that we do not understand Allah's program, we can only know certain things. When we become closer to Allah, when we know about Allah, when we know what Allah wants from us, then we increase our self in knowledge and freedoms.

The more knowledge we have, the more freedom we have. If you are sitting at the airport, you will be different than the person sitting in the street or the market regarding the knowledge of when the airplanes are taking off and landing. You could look at the arrivals and departures screens and know which planes are coming from which countries and which planes are going where because you have "insider information" because you are there.

Now, if someone were to take you to the control tower, you would be able to see everything in greater detail and if someone were to take you, for example, to Pine Gap, your information and knowledge would increase again, dramatically. The closer you are to the Source of Knowledge, the better you see things, the more clearly you see the events in your life, the lives of others, and even world events. Not all the information that one may receive is what could be considered to be pleasant. When you have access to higher knowledge, then you are never really surprised. You become calmer and more tranquil because you know that everything is in the Hands of Allah and under His control.

If we are closer to Allah, see with the eyes of Allah, and know with the knowledge of Allah, then nothing will really disturb us. We will be spontaneous, we will be peaceful, and we know that whatever Allah does is not like the activities that go on at Pine Gap but is for the benefit of everyone - not to harm anyone, but for the benefit of everyone.

People may ask, "Why does Allah starve people in some places and let people make war in other places?" Humanity can learn from these events and perhaps wake up a little bit and activate the compassion within them. For example, in our times, nobody wants to get old anymore. As soon as people begin to lose some of their looks, advance in age, or perhaps become ill, they are considered to be useless and so many even want to commit suicide to remove their burden from society. There has been a push for some time to legalise euthanasia.

This is very wrong and deprives humanity of the function of becoming old. Old people have the potential to activate compassion, caring, and love in humanity. When you see an old person or someone who is sick, it should bring about the realisation within us that one day we will be like this and activate our desire to do what we can to help.

Although now, we must be very careful about helping because so many people refuse assistance and may get angry with you and cause difficulties for you. The trust between people has suffered so much over the years and it has become risky to help. This loss of trust has also created the atmosphere of over-legislation. People do not trust each other, and they do not trust themselves to do the right thing, so, rather than speak up or take appropriate action, they respond by making yet another law. People who are awake and conscious don't need laws to tell them what to do and what not to do because they are naturally self-regulating.

Deterioration of Human Society

Excessive law making and legislation is an indication of the deterioration of the condition of humanity. So many things should come automatically because of our human nature, our natural way of helping one another, and being kind to one another. If something is not right, it's not right and you should have developed the will to avoid it if it is not good. There are so many things we really shouldn't need to make laws for. If we are decent human beings, we shouldn't commit wrongdoing in the first place. The will of humans is not there anymore, so many people are full of desires and have no self-control.

Fifty years ago, it was rare to see someone running in the street unless he was a thief or a criminal. Now, people are running everywhere and it's all okay. In their shorts, headphones in, isolating them further. So, they eat, run, run, eat, and so the cycle continues. This is called "enjoying life," eat, run, work, sleep, and back to work. People are so busy (and selfish) now that for many, procreation is not in their program anymore. Having children is something that many people don't have time for and the process itself has become mixed up. If we look at things now, it's not the doomsday scenario people speak of; it has gone beyond that.

Grandmothers carrying babies for their daughters, daughters carrying children for their brothers, women getting paid for being a surrogate and carrying a child that is not related to her at all. This causes the breaking of society because the psyche is a very fragile thing. The bond between mother and child is very strong; even if a woman carries a child knowing that the child is not hers, that bond is still made. It has the potential to create very serious problems and complications when people do something like this, even though the intention to help someone may be true. Family relationships can become confused as well. For example, if a grandmother is carrying a child for her daughter, how is that child going to be related to the grandmother and to any other children in the family?

Sometimes we end up making things more complicated and confused when we try to fix things. In this case another person's infertility, because from there it wasn't such a large step for women to hire another woman to carry her child because she is too busy or doesn't want to "ruin her body." The whole program is upside down and this is very dangerous.

Anyone who is serious and really takes genuine steps towards Allah will receive plenty. The supermarket of Allah has no customers; the shelves are full, but everyone is looking out for number one (his own self). Allah says, "I am here, I could give you everything," but nobody wants anything from Allah. If anyone takes one step towards Him, he says, "I come running towards you."

Question 25 – Consume that Which is Pure

As humans, we drink water, eat meat and grains, and in particular, what comes to mind from the teaching is milk and honey. Is there anything else quite like milk and honey?

There are several foods mentioned in the Holy Qur'an, fruits in general and specifically dates, grapes, pomegranates, meats such as fowl and cattle, grains, and grasses. Allah says in the Holy Qur'an:

مَّثَلُ ٱلْجَنَّةِ ٱلَّتِى وُعِدَ ٱلْمُتَّقُونَ فِيهَآ أَنْهَـٰرٌ مِّن مَّآءٍ غَيْرِ
ءَاسِنٍ وَأَنْهَـٰرٌ مِّن لَّبَنٍ لَّمْ يَتَغَيَّرْ طَعْمُهُۥ وَأَنْهَـٰرٌ مِّنْ خَمْرٍ
لَّذَّةٍ لِّلشَّـٰرِبِينَ وَأَنْهَـٰرٌ مِّنْ عَسَلٍ مُّصَفًّى وَلَهُمْ فِيهَا مِن كُلِّ
ٱلثَّمَرَٰتِ وَمَغْفِرَةٌ مِّن رَّبِّهِمْ

(Here is) a Parable of the Garden which the righteous are promised: in it are rivers of water incorruptible; rivers of milk of which the taste never changes; rivers of wine, a joy to those

who drink; and rivers of honey pure and clear. In it there are for them all kinds of fruits; and Grace from their Lord
(Holy Qur'an 47:15)

The two you asked of - milk and honey - are both spiritually significant and highly nutritious. Honey is collected from all types of plants and nectars, and milk is produced from all types of grasses. If you have a glass of milk with honey, then you basically have everything.

So, in a sense, the honey is a condensation of the vegetable kingdom and the milk is a condensation of the animal kingdom?

Yes! And we just spend our time stuffing ourselves with food for the body when there is so much more. There is also the food of impressions, which can either be spiritually nutritious or detrimental. What we put into our hearts and minds needs to be refined. If you were to go to the ocean or to the forest, you would hear beautiful sounds and see the birds and this brings a beautiful feeling to your heart. But, if you go to the rubbish tip and fill yourself with the sounds and smells there and all the flies, you are not going to think it is very nice. The impressions created by these two scenarios are quite different. So, one has to be selective. Sometimes, you may go somewhere and just feel like you are being strangled and you need to exit immediately. This is because the energy flow and conditions in that place are not conducive to your spiritual elevation. This is why you should seek Allah in the nicer places.

Love Thy Neighbour

One time, when Christ عليه السلام was walking with his disciples, they passed a dead dog, rotten and stinking. They all said, "What a horrible smell" and each was saying something or another about the condition of this dog. But the Holy Prophet Jesus Christ عليه السلام said, "What beautiful white teeth he has." He was able to see the beauty in an unpleasant situation and some of us may be able to see the nice things in the midst of something rotten, but most are not, so it's better to be careful where you go. When someone does something bad to you, as a traveller on the Path, you must remember that he has a spirit within him. So, you may not like his actions as such, but you have to like him inside, because Allah is within him the same as He is within you.

With regards to the saying "love thy neighbour" – The Holy Prophet ﷺ related that the Archangel Gabriel عَلَيْهِ السَّلَامُ was telling him to love his neighbour so much that he thought he was going to make his neighbour inherit him. That's how serious this is. If you love Allah and Allah is in everyone, then you must love your neighbour because Allah is in him. You are not loving your neighbour in the sense of a physical love, but in a spiritual way because you are loving Allah which is within him. Sometimes you could get a very rotten neighbour and it's difficult to find Allah in him, so you do have to be careful implementing some of the things that we speak of here, because they belong to a higher state of consciousness and awareness.

The first stage is that one should not do wrong things to others. Forget about doing good to anyone, just don't harm anyone. Then, if you master the art of not doing bad things, you are able to look back at some point and see that you have not done anything bad for a period, then you say

Alhamdulillah, "All Praise is due to Allah." You thank Allah for purifying your actions. Then you could start to do a little bit of good, you could start to help people a little bit. After you master this helping stage, then you begin to accept the bad that they do to you – when you do nice things for people, and they do bad things to you in return. This is the difficult part. Allah really wants to test your sincerity here. Are you truly full of awareness, consciousness, and love of Allah? Are you doing good for the sake of Allah, or for the sake of your own self? If you do wonderful things and they tell you to get lost, or that they didn't ask for your help, and you feel this in your heart, then you are false. You are still thinking that you are the doer, when, it is really Allah that is the doer. If you are thinking that Allah is within you and He is telling you to help the other person, who also has Allah within him, then here you are talking to Allah in general. Allah does, and Allah rejects, and you are caught between. If you feel upset about this and declare that you are not going to help this ungrateful person anymore, that means that you are not quite there yet. One should help as much as he can tolerate, but you must also be careful. The conditions of the people are very necessary and you should be aware of this. It is good to do things without expectation of a reward.

The best step towards enlightenment is to do something good for someone that you are never going to see again.

Question 26 – The Source of Knowledge

What is the Source of your Knowledge?

Our knowledge comes from the Holy Qur'an, the final message of Allah to the creations and from the *sunnah* (the words and actions) of the Holy Prophet Muhammad ﷺ.

Question 27 – Annihilation (*Fana'*)

What is *Fana'* and How is it Achieved?

Fana' is self-annihilation, or self-effacement, or dissolution, or passing away from self. Through being joined to Allah, the Real, man is annihilated from himself - the "limited existence" of the traveller is overpowered by the "absolute existence" of Allah, so that the traveller becomes unaware of his own self and the creation. *Fana'* is the last stage on the ascent to Allah. When travelling to the Source, the seeker passes through different levels of *fana'*, each of which brings him closer to his Goal. There are hundreds, even thousands, of *fana'*. Every time a form of ignorance is removed to be replaced by knowledge the *murid* has experienced *fana'*. Every time you transform a negative quality into a positive quality, this is considered to be a form of *fana'*. He has tasted the annihilation of an ignorance. This doesn't happen "all in one blast," but step by step as the *murid* changes and transforms the qualities of his being. The first stage of *fana'* is the most difficult because one has to face himself and face the truth about his short comings, but as one progresses, acceptance comes.

Every moment of existence is in fact a moment which is pregnant - infused with its own particular knowledge. So, for the aware one, each moment can be a *fana'*. However, within the higher teaching of *tasawwuf,* there are three major types of *fana'*, through which the *murid* must travel if he is to reach the Absolute. These are Annihilation in the Murshid/Spiritual Guide, Annihilation in the Messenger, and Annihilation in Allah. When true *fana'* is experienced, it is beyond the personality and beyond the self. Experience of the Essence is an experience of the Truth Itself.

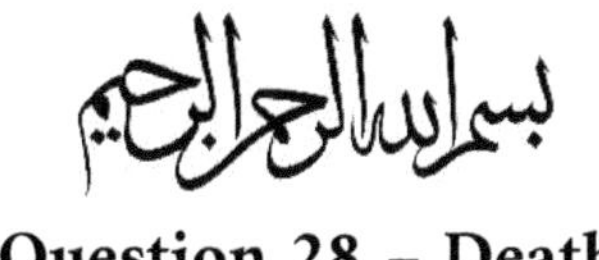

Question 28 – Death

What Happens when a Person Dies?

There are many things that happen during the dying process, but we do not generally see them. Firstly, the person's actions will manifest themselves, but most importantly is the element of nature which is keeping him alive. There is the angel who is trusted with his breathing - who will come to him and say, "I have searched heaven and earth, looking for one breath that is destined for you, but I could not find any more." The angel in trust of his food will come to him and say, "I have looked everywhere for even one grain of rice that is written for you, but there is none left." The same for the angel who is entrusted with his water - not one drop left. When these destined provisions are used, that's the end of the program and the person must face a new level of consciousness.

At that point, this life becomes the dream and the next life becomes the interpretation of that dream. If you look back from the other realm and see yourself in a state of prayer, a state of Remembrance of Allah, a state of joy with Allah, then the interpretation of your dream will be wonderful. But if you see yourself busy with other things, then you will see the interpretation in another way.

We will all meet Allah and we are moving towards that meeting every moment of our lives. Allah says:

يَـٰٓأَيُّهَا ٱلْإِنسَـٰنُ إِنَّكَ كَادِحٌ إِلَىٰ رَبِّكَ كَدْحًا فَمُلَـٰقِيهِ

You, verily, O man, are striving toward your Lord - a work which you will meet (in His presence)
(Holy Qur'an 84:6)

Everyone must meet Allah, but that meeting can be either a pleasant meeting or a dangerous meeting. You could be standing there with chains or your feet or you could be in a beautiful coach entering the presence of the King.

Question 29 – Fear (*khawf*)

Why do People Live in Fear?

Allah says in the Holy Qur'an:

أَلَآ إِنَّ أَوْلِيَآءَ ٱللَّهِ لَا خَوْفٌ عَلَيْهِمْ وَلَا هُمْ يَحْزَنُونَ

Behold! Verily on the friends of Allah there is no fear, nor shall they grieve

(Holy Qur'an 10:62)

Malik ibn Dinar ﵁ was a great Master from Baghdad. He was walking through the streets during a time of famine. He came across a young girl who was happily skipping rope. He stopped and he asked of her, "Are you not worried about the famine?" And she said to him, "Oh no, my Master has plenty of food." Suddenly the realisation hit him, right there and then, like a silver bullet, and he started to cry. If we had the realisation that Allah has plenty of "food," we would never worry about anything.

Because our thoughts are fixed on material things, we have worries in our lives. The Holy Prophet ﷺ said, "Whoever fears something, Allah will fix it upon him." So, if we fear hunger, Allah creates famine. If we fear drowning, Allah puts us in the sea. If we fear gangsters, every corner we turn, there is someone. If we fear war, then war comes from every direction. People fear disease and we certainly have them by the tonne. Every week there's a new list. So, everything that humanity is afraid of, they get.

The reason for this is that they have no fear of Allah Most High. If the fear of the human was centred on One, Allah, then everything will be subjugated to you. As Allah said in the Holy Qur'an:

وَسَخَّرَ لَكُم مَّا فِى ٱلسَّمَٰوَٰتِ وَمَا فِى ٱلْأَرْضِ جَمِيعًا مِّنْهُ
إِنَّ فِى ذَٰلِكَ لَءَايَٰتٍ لِّقَوْمٍ يَتَفَكَّرُونَ

And He has subjected to you, as from Him, all that is in the heavens and on earth: Behold, in that are Signs indeed for those who reflect

(Holy Qur'an 45:13)

Because we fear "other than Allah" in our weak way of understanding things, we live in fear. This is why Malik ibn Dinar ﵀ began to cry, because he saw the little girl as having complete trust in her Master while everyone else was worried about bread.

Question 30 – Knowledge and Gnosis

What is the difference between knowledge and gnosis?

Imam al-Ghazali says, in *The letters of Imam al Ghazali*, "gnosis is the nearness of the self and the realisations of the heart. Because of that, the affect of *ma'rifa* (Divine knowledge or gnosis) will be manifested in the rest of the body. If knowledge is like fire, then gnosis is the heat which comes out of the fire." *Ma'rifa* is a light which Allah casts into the heart of whomsoever He Wills. This is the true knowledge which comes through unveiling, witnessing, and tasting. This knowledge is from Allah, it is not Allah Himself, because He Is Unknowable in His Essence. The triad on the Sufi Path of Return is comprised of Fear, Knowledge, and Love. Fear leads to Knowledge, which leads to Unconditional Love of Allah. It is said that spiritual struggle is child's play while *ma'rifa* is men's work. So, if you have knowledge but you receive no warmth from it, then it is not beneficial to you. The Holy Prophet ﷺ said, "Oh Allah, I take refuge in You from knowledge which brings no benefit" (*Sahih Muslim*). Any knowledge is just that - knowledge. If you know how to make a cup, that is knowledge. Even witchcraft is knowledge, but it is not going to bring you closer to salvation. It will not take you closer to Allah.

Gnosis is knowledge of Allah, His Attributes, and His Essence, without any doubts whatsoever - this is gnosis. Others from the People of Allah have confirmed this by saying that gnosis is knowledge of the Attributes and the Essence of Allah.

Question 31 – Paradise

When we are in this life, we strive to overcome our thoughts, passions, and desires for anything "other than Allah." When we transition to the other side, does the same apply? Do we still need to purify our desires within our own "Paradise" until there is nothing left to desire but Allah?

Yes, most definitely. The purification process, *insha'Allah,* begins in this life. Through the practices of the teaching of the Holy Prophet Muhammad ﷺ and the Remembrance of Allah, the *murid* will travel through different levels of the purification process. When we pass on from this realm and, *insha'Allah,* enter our own Paradise, it will be filled with those things that we love, people, places, foods - really, anything that we desire. For most people, this is the reward for their striving in this life. There are, however, people whose ultimate desire and aim is Allah, and Allah only. For these folk, the purification process continues.

The Messenger of God ﷺ said, "In Paradise, God, ever exalted is He, says to the people of Paradise, 'I am Allah, the One who gives lavishly, the Rich beyond need, the One who fulfils His promise perfectly, the wholly Truthful. This is My abode and I have let you dwell here. This is My Garden and I have granted you complete access to it. This is My Self and I have let you see Me. Here is My Hand, which holds the dew and the rain, generously spread out over you, without ever being kept from you. And I, I gaze upon you, without ever turning My Eyes away from you. So, ask Me whatever you wish and desire. I have made you intimate with Myself, I am the One who is sitting with you, delighting in your company. Never more shall there be need or want, suffering or misery, weakness or old age, discontent or oppression, nor shall this ever be changed for all eternity. The bounty of Eternity is your felicity. You are those who rest in security and permanently abide in eternal existence, the ennobled, the blessed! You are the most noble lords, who have been obedient to Me and have avoided My prohibitions. So bring your needs to me. Let Me satisfy them for you, with generosity and munificence.' They reply, 'Our Lord, it is not this that we hoped and longed for. What we want of You is the sight of Your Generous Face for all eternity, and Your good-pleasure with us.' The High, the Supreme, the King of the kingdom, the One who gives most lavishly and generously, ever blessed and exalted is He, says to them, 'This is My Face, which discloses Itself to you forever and ever. Rejoice! For I Myself am well-pleased with you. Enjoy!'" (*Mishkat al-Anwar*).

The choice is there for us - we can enjoy our state of bliss and all that it contains - everything that Allah has promised us in the Holy Qur'an and more than we could ever imagine - or continue the journey and strive for the ultimate goal of perpetual bliss in the never-ending presence of the Divine. There is a verse in the Holy Qur'an that, when recited by Allah Almighty Himself will put the people who hear it into a state of ecstasy for 40,000 years.

Question 32 – Stages of Development

What are some of the different stages of development that a *murid* may pass through and what are the indications of these?

Ahh, this is a very big question which requires a lengthy answer. For the moment, it will suffice to say that in the beginning of your travel, it is important to try not to advise others or to correct their faults. It is a trick of the ego-self to think that you have something to offer and are capable of advising others. The Holy Prophet ﷺ said, "Whoever keeps silence, will be safe" (*Jami' al-Tirmidhi*). One of the Companions of The Holy Prophet ﷺ, 'Umar رضي الله عنه, said, "May Allah have mercy on anyone who shows me the faults of my self." He used to get very happy if someone pointed out his shortcomings. However, this is, of course a very special art – you cannot just go around telling people their faults. The sign that they are not ready to accept is that as soon as you tell them, they will begin attacking you.

In the beginning, your business is to keep control of your own self and to improve her state and particularly, do not do any harm to others. Never mind about doing good to others, just don't do any harm to them. That, in itself, is a tremendous action. Next, you try to accept some of their faults and wrong actions towards you and *then* you may begin to do some good towards them as well. Allah says in the Holy Qur'an:

وَجَزَٰٓؤُا۟ سَيِّئَةٍ سَيِّئَةٌ مِّثْلُهَا فَمَنْ عَفَا وَأَصْلَحَ فَأَجْرُهُۥ عَلَى ٱللَّهِ

The recompense for an injury is an injury equal thereto (in degree): but if a person forgives and makes reconciliation, his reward is due from Allah.

(Holy Qur'an 42:40)

وَٱلْعَافِينَ عَنِ ٱلنَّاسِ وَٱللَّهُ يُحِبُّ ٱلْمُحْسِنِينَ

And pardon (all) men; for Allah loves those who do good

(Holy Qur'an 3:134)

So, when a wrong action is done to you, you could retaliate (teaching of the Torah/Moses عَلَيْهِ السَّلَامُ), you could forgive (Gospel/Jesus عَلَيْهِ السَّلَامُ), or you could go above all of that and be perfect within yourself (Qur'an/Holy Prophet Muhammad ﷺ). Take a lesson from that particular experience, improve your understanding, and ensure that you do not do the same to others in the future.

بسم الله الرحمن الرحيم

Question 33 – The Day of *Alast*

What is the Sufi Interpretation of the Verse:

وَإِذْ أَخَذَ رَبُّكَ مِنۢ بَنِىٓ ءَادَمَ مِن ظُهُورِهِمْ ذُرِّيَّتَهُمْ
وَأَشْهَدَهُمْ عَلَىٰٓ أَنفُسِهِمْ أَلَسْتُ بِرَبِّكُمْ قَالُوا۟ بَلَىٰ شَهِدْنَآ أَن
تَقُولُوا۟ يَوْمَ ٱلْقِيَـٰمَةِ إِنَّا كُنَّا عَنْ هَـٰذَا غَـٰفِلِينَ

When your Lord drew forth from the Children of Adam - from their loins - their descendants, and made them testify concerning themselves, (saying): "Am I not your Lord (who cherishes and sustains you)?"- They said: "Yea! We do testify!" (This), lest you should say on the Day of Judgment: "Of this we were unaware."

(Holy Qur'an 7:172)

In parts of North Africa, when a person is asked, "How long have you known so and so?" He may reply, "Since the day of *alastu Birubbikum*." This is a reference to the above verse of the Holy Qur'an, and indicates that the two were acquainted in the world of the spirit. At certain times in our life we may meet someone and it feels as if we have known them forever, even though we have only just met. This feeling of affinity between two people can be attributed to being in close proximity on that Day of *alast*. When the two meet in this realm, there is something in their spirits which recognise each other even though they may not be consciously aware of the reason for their affinity. This is also known as the second manifestation of the spirit. Initially, the spirits are in the essence of Allah without any specific identity except in the consciousness of Allah. The second stage of manifestation is when the spirits have their own identity.

When Allah spoke in the realm of the spirit, a shower of celestial light descended on the spirits. Those who were in closer proximity to the source of that light became the Prophets, Messengers, and Saints. Then there are those who were not quite so close to the centre of the descent, and this accounts for the different levels of awareness of humanity. Those who were close to each other in the world of the spirit will have a certain affinity in this realm as well. When two people meet in this realm, their spirits reach out and interact with each other. If that affinity is there, they will feel close to each other and if it is not, they will be neutral or repel each other. Through unveiling, this action of the spirits can be witnessed.

The problem with humanity comes when the spirit descends to this realm and is encased in the body. We then become subject to forgetfulness and relapse. We forget that state of consciousness when we were fully aware in the presence of our Lord. This is why so many Prophets and Messengers were sent to remind us – not to tell us – but to remind us to return to the Source and acknowledge God.

Question 34 – What Allah Wants

What does Allah really want from the Human?

What Allah really wants from this human being is belief. Amazingly enough, belief comes in so many varieties. We have had people sitting with us earlier who were Hindus, Muslims, and Christians. Each one of them has their belief. In the real sense their belief could be a wrong belief, but it is still a belief. Even people who are wrong are very firm in their wrongness. Even a person who says he is an Atheist really believes that he is an Atheist and this is still a form of belief.

The greatest thing that one could believe in is Unity. Belief is one thing, but how to get closer to the Unity, which is Allah - this is where you begin to have felicity, you begin to have happiness and solace, you begin to have illumination. This is the difference between accurate and inaccurate knowledge of the Unity of Allah. Allah says in the Holy Qur'an:

أَفِي ٱللَّهِ شَكٌّ فَاطِرِ ٱلسَّمَـٰوَٰتِ وَٱلْأَرْضِ

Is there a doubt about Allah, The Creator of the heavens and the earth?

(Holy Qur'an 14:10)

For man to create something, he first has to create himself from nothing, but nothing cannot create anything, it could only create nothing. So, to deny the existence of a Creator, Allah, and you don't see Allah's hand in everything, this is very sad. *Allah is the Creator of the heavens and the earth*. And *It is Allah who created you from nothing*. *Allah is the Light of the Heavens and the Earth*. These are all verses from the Holy Qur'an concerning the creation and the Creator. The more you focus on the Source, Allah, then you find that you are happier, and the mind and the personality will come under the control and direction of the spiritual self.

Question 35 – Connection to Allah

How does one achieve this connection to Allah?

Contemplation is a great portion of this. Firstly, you have to be 100% certain of Allah. That He is the Master of all things. You could think about Allah as *al-Rahman, al-Raheem* (the Compassionate, the Merciful) or any other of His Names, but this will take you out of the very key of focus. To focus is to focus on Allah. The Name "Allah" is the *ism al-Jami'ah,* the Name that gathers together all the Names. When they asked the Holy Prophet ﷺ when the world will end, he replied, "When there is no one left who says 'Allah'" (*Sahih Muslim*). When you say "Allah," you are keeping the creation alive. We have spoken of this before, so when one sits in contemplation, focus on the Name "Allah" in your imagination. Close your eyes and try to picture it. It doesn't matter how many times it slips away, just try to bring it back again. Keep practicing this and, eventually, the Name will stay there. Do this while you make *dhikr* of the Name "Allah." Just "Allah" and nothing else, quietly to yourself. Then this will become the focus of your thoughts and there is no interpretation necessary.

Now, that is one. The other, and this is only to help you and assist you to develop your connection with Allah Most High. This second stage may cause a little bit of fear. One must be very certain that nothing can harm him because he is connected to Allah. And that is to imagine light as well. As you make *dhikr* of the Name "Allah," you imagine sitting in that light, that everything is made of that light. Allah said He is the Light of the heavens and the earth. First, one imagines the Name and focuses on that. Now you have the Name, you can focus and have control of it.

Next you begin to see that this Light surrounds you and goes around you and through your body. Then you will be able to see it moving to a longer distance and eventually you may be able to connect with other things. Where there is Light you will be able to move things with that Light. In the lower grade, you could say that this is the Chi. In the higher grade this is the Power of Allah. This is the Source of happiness, the Source of seeing Reality in its flow. This is a flowing reality, not a stationary reality.

The Essence of Allah moves like a river without limitations, without boundaries and without ceasing. It is constantly moving and this is the flow of the life-force of Allah, Glorified and Most Exalted is He. As I said, the first thing is to make *dhikr* of the Name "Allah." Do it by yourself, quietly to yourself, you could do it with the breath and also it is sometimes mentioned as the "circulation of the *dhikr*." When the Name is stable and stopped in your forehead, you will be able to move it around your body and direct it to wherever you want by the power of your thoughts, your imagination. Imagination is also part of the creation itself. By practising this for a half an hour and completing the practices outlined - you could sit and see with your eyes closed. This is Light. Before, probably people used to question - how, why, what for, but now we know and science tells us that everything is made of light. Electrons, quarks, and atoms, they are all a flow of light.

You are not looking for atoms and photons and this sort of thing, you are aiming for the Source of Light.

When your real imagination becomes activated, you could transport yourself within that Light and go to the Ka'aba for example. This is where people may say to you things like "I felt your presence," "I thought you were there," and "I could smell you and I looked around for you." This is part of the spiritual projection of Light. As I said, it is required for us to eliminate the chatter of the mind, any negative contemplation on past things – "what if" stuff that is gone. And things that cause you remorse. These things all have to be neutralised and eliminated before you can progress further on the Path of Allah. Then you start to work on the Real things and then, when you examine yourself at the end of the day, you will not find any mistakes or wrongdoings in your actions, no gaps, just a straight flow of beauty in your day, whatever you are doing. *Alhamdulillah,* you will become in a state of harmony with the Divine Beauty. Allah is beautiful and He loves beauty. There is nothing ugly in that realm. This is the sharpness of the Unity of

Allah and this is a very huge and tremendously powerful step that we have just talked about. This is the highest worship. Allah says:

قُلِ ٱللَّهُ ثُمَّ ذَرْهُمْ فِى خَوْضِهِمْ يَلْعَبُونَ

Say Allah, and leave them to their vain prattling

(Holy Qur'an 6:91)

Question 36 – Good and Negative Actions

What is the Meaning of the Verse:

ظَهَرَ ٱلْفَسَادُ فِى ٱلْبَرِّ وَٱلْبَحْرِ بِمَا كَسَبَتْ أَيْدِى ٱلنَّاسِ
لِيُذِيقَهُم بَعْضَ ٱلَّذِى عَمِلُوا۟ لَعَلَّهُمْ يَرْجِعُونَ

Corruption has appeared on land and in the sea as an outcome of what men's hands have wrought: and so He will let them taste [the evil of] some of their doings, so that they might return [to the right path]

(Holy Qur'an 30:41)

Allah is good and whatever He does is good, but mankind has taken it upon their own selves to commit negative actions which has brought on an increased corruption on the earth. This harm comes not only as a direct consequence of the actions committed, but also as a reprimand or punishment from Allah. Not only is the earth affected by the mischief and evil that is wrought upon her, but the oceans, seas, and other waterways are also affected. If we look at this symbolically, we can see that the earth is related to our bodies, which are our outer selves and the sea to our inner, spiritual selves. Shaykh Abu Yazid al-Bistami ﷺ said, "The greatest signs of the People of Allah are that you see them carrying on their daily lives like other people, but their hearts are in total peace and tranquillity with the Divine, in the Holy Fold." No matter what happens in their lives, the connection with Allah has been made and it is constant, so they do not get disturbed by exterior happenings.

We can compare this connection with the Divine Light and Energy to an electrical appliance that we can plug in, in order to make it work. Let's say the vacuum cleaner. We plug it in and begin to use it, but when we reach the end of the cord, if we continue, we lose the connection and have to walk all the way back and either get an extension cord or plug in to a new socket. However, once you make that link with Allah, that's it. It doesn't matter where you go, Allah says "I am with you" (see Holy Qur'an 57:4) and:

وَنَحْنُ أَقْرَبُ إِلَيْهِ مِنْ حَبْلِ ٱلْوَرِيدِ

We are closer to you than your jugular vein

(Holy Qur'an 50:16)

وَفِىٓ أَنفُسِكُمْ أَفَلَا تُبْصِرُونَ

It is within you, can you not see

(Holy Qur'an 51:21)

The problem with humanity is that state of forgetfulness, the state of absent-mindedness. Shaykh al-'Alawi رَحِمَهُ ٱللَّهُ said, "The one who is the worshipper and the theologian is no good in the company of the people who receive directly from Allah." When you are in their company and you speak of such things that we speak of here, they will object and they will cause a disturbance in the flow of energy and this could actually cause harm to him, so it is better not to engage with this type of person in the first place.

The theologian looks at the Qur'an from the perspective of what Allah wants from him, not in order to know Allah.

He wants to know *halal* and *haram,* where he can know "I can do this" and "I cannot do that." The distance between the darkness and the light, where we say there is no darkness - it is just a state of forgetfulness.

Allah says, "When I love him, I become his eyes that he sees with, his tongue that he speaks with, his hand with which he grasps, his ears that he hears with and his feet which he walks with," in other words, "I become him." So, where is the darkness? There is no darkness. The darkness that we perceive is only a state of forgetfulness. Your self comes in between like the moon during the eclipse of the sun, blocking out the light. The self has no consciousness of her worth and thinks differently. One of the tools to achieving spiritual success and happiness is, of course to neutralise the self. We are not talking here about the lowest stage of the self, the ego-self, the criminal-self, but the second stage, the complaining-self, the one that has a measure of consciousness. This self looks to the right and sees angels and to the left and sees the demons and is drawn towards the angels and the light. Once you make the choice for the angelic side, the development of the spiritual side, you are saved from the negative things, become peaceful, and you begin to see the beautiful manifestations of Allah.

Question 37 – The *'Arif* and the *Mu'min*

What is the Difference between the *'Arif*, the one who knows, and the *Mu'min*, the one who believes?

We have to understand that one's state of illumination is based upon how much you know of yourself and how much you know of Allah, Most High. You cannot know nothing and then expect to receive plenty from the bounty of Allah. It's amazing that we all know this in our normal day to day lives, in our work, and the organisation of our lives, but when it comes to spiritual teaching, their personal relationship with God, people don't seem to get that it takes a certain amount of effort to achieve. Anyway, the difference between the one who believes and the one who knows is that the one who knows sees by the Light of Allah. The Holy Prophet ﷺ said, "Be aware of the *firasa,* the clear sight and the telepathic power of the believer, because he sees with the light of Allah" (*Jami' al-Tirmidhi*). Now, the one who has the higher knowledge, does he see with the same light? No, he sees "by God," "by Allah." This is different, one sees with the Light of Allah, that manifestation of light and he is connected to it. He doesn't really know how it works, but he knows that there is something powerful there. The other one, he sees "by Allah" with a fuller understanding.

The believer has a heart and his heart comes to a state of tranquillity and peace with the remembrance of Allah. The one who knows becomes tranquil "in Allah." The Holy Prophet ﷺ said this world is the prison of the believer, but for those who know are in a state of thankfulness. The believer is in prison because, while he believes, he does not have the higher knowledge required in order to free himself from attachments and to understand what is behind the actions. The Prophet Jesus عَلَيْهِ ٱلسَّلَامُ said that if someone hits you on your cheek, you give him the other one. The reasoning behind this, if you are a man of knowledge, is that you recognise that the one doing the hitting is not the other person, but it is, in fact, Allah that hit you in the face. So, your thinking is that you must have done something wrong so you turn your face to present the other side (to get balanced).

Those who know the higher knowledge of Allah are in a state of thankfulness and they are absent from the presence of the material world. Their Lord has given them the drink of His Love and His Presence and He has also given them the drink of longing for Him. Imam al-Junayd رحمه الله said, "We drank the wine of Love, before the creation of the grapes." Just so people don't get confused as to which sort of wine they are drinking, this is the Divine Nectar. This "drink," or "link" if you want to call it, is the drink of the state of forgetfulness with regard to the creations and the awakening with Allah. Remember how before you were in a state of absentmindedness and forgetfulness in the material world, but now you are in a state of forgetfulness in a different way. You no longer see the creations as you did before. They are still there, you see them, but your link with them is in a different way altogether.

The one who knows the realities of Allah has realised and truly knows that it is Allah Who has created everything. It is incorrect to think that Allah has created everything and then separated Himself from it, just to let it tick along on its own. This is a state of separation in your thinking.

When the Prophet Moses ﷺ was summoned to the meeting with Allah, Allah showed him many miracles. Yet, when he was told to go to the Pharaoh with the signs he was given, he was afraid because of wrongdoing that he had previously committed in the land. Allah said to him:

لَا تَخَافَآ إِنَّنِى مَعَكُمَآ أَسْمَعُ وَأَرَىٰ

Fear not: for I am with you: I hear and see (*everything*)
(Holy Qur'an 20:46)

This is why the Companions of the Holy Prophet ﷺ were so unique - they didn't see water, they didn't see rocks, they saw Allah in everything. They did what they needed to and then moved on without attachment. After the Prophets and Messengers, they are the most unique human beings. They knew in their hearts all they needed to know, and they were privileged to be in the presence of the Universal Man, the Holy Prophet Muhammad ﷺ, the Seal of Messagehood and Prophethood.

بسم الله الرحمن الرحيم

Question 38 – The People of the Cave

Who are the "People of the Cave" in *Surah al-Kahf*?

Many of the Companions of the Holy Prophet Muhammad ﷺ were very poor and, while he loved them all very much, he also wanted to attract the others to Islam and was spending time with them. One of the Companions suggested these other people should be removed so that the Holy Prophet ﷺ could spend more time with them. When the Holy Prophet ﷺ replied and asked to be left alone while he spoke with the others, this verse was revealed to him immediately:

وَٱصْبِرْ نَفْسَكَ مَعَ ٱلَّذِينَ يَدْعُونَ رَبَّهُم بِٱلْغَدَوٰةِ وَٱلْعَشِىِّ
يُرِيدُونَ وَجْهَهُۥ وَلَا تَعْدُ عَيْنَاكَ عَنْهُمْ تُرِيدُ زِينَةَ ٱلْحَيَوٰةِ
ٱلدُّنْيَا وَلَا تُطِعْ مَنْ أَغْفَلْنَا قَلْبَهُۥ عَن ذِكْرِنَا وَٱتَّبَعَ هَوَىٰهُ
وَكَانَ أَمْرُهُۥ فُرُطًا

And keep yourself content with those who call on their Lord morning and evening, seeking His Face; and let not your eyes pass beyond them, seeking the pomp and glitter of this Life, nor obey any whose heart We have permitted to neglect the remembrance of Us, one who follows his own desires, whose case has gone beyond all bounds

(Holy Qur'an 18:28)

The Holy Prophet ﷺ was in such a state after the revelation of this verse, that, when he sat with his companions, he would never turn his face away from them or leave them. Until either Abu Bakr رضي الله عنه or Umar رضي الله عنه would tell them that they should move on and allow the Holy Prophet ﷺ to go about his other business.

وَقُلِ ٱلْحَقُّ مِن رَّبِّكُمْ فَمَن شَآءَ فَلْيُؤْمِن وَمَن شَآءَ فَلْيَكْفُرْ

And say: "The truth [has now come] from your Sustainer: let, then, him who wills, believe in it, and let him who wills, reject it"

(Holy Qur'an 18:29)

This is why Allah sometimes gives us this concept of "anyone who wills," so that we know we each have responsibility for our own selves when we stand before Allah on the Day of Judgement. No one can say, "I was forced." Regarding those people who take false gods and worship things as the Sun and the Moon and the stars: when the life force is taken from them, they will be thrown into Hell. This is just to show that they are not gods, because if they were, they would not allow themselves to be overthrown.

There is an amazing complexity in the teaching of Allah.

وَتَحْسَبُهُمْ أَيْقَاظًا وَهُمْ رُقُودٌ وَنُقَلِّبُهُمْ ذَاتَ ٱلْيَمِينِ وَذَاتَ
ٱلشِّمَالِ وَكَلْبُهُم بَٰسِطٌ ذِرَاعَيْهِ بِٱلْوَصِيدِ لَوِ ٱطَّلَعْتَ عَلَيْهِمْ
لَوَلَّيْتَ مِنْهُمْ فِرَارًا وَلَمُلِئْتَ مِنْهُمْ رُعْبًا

You would have thought they were awake, while they were asleep, and We turned them on their right and on their left sides: their dog stretching forth his two forelegs on the threshold: if you had come up on to them, you would have certainly turned back from them in flight, and would certainly have been filled with terror of them

(Holy Qur'an 18:18)

This is because they were in a different station (*maqam*). Allah held them in that state for over 300 years. Always, the miracles of Allah, Glorified and Most Exalted is He, creates a certain energy that changes the atmosphere of the area and opens up to a different celestial realm. If you do not belong to that particular realm, then fear and terror will overtake you. Either fear that you will be pulled towards them or pulled away from them.

And the other one, of course, is

وَلَا تَقُولَنَّ لِشَاْىْءٍ إِنِّى فَاعِلٌ ذَٰلِكَ غَدًا

إِلَّآ أَن يَشَآءَ ٱللَّهُ

And do not say of anything, "I shall be sure to do so and so tomorrow" - without (adding), "if God so wills"

(Holy Qur'an 18:23-24)

You should always say *insha'Allah* – if Allah wills. By doing this, you are connecting your will to Allah's will. So you make your plans and say *insha'Allah*. *And remember your Lord when you forget. If you forget everything else, then remember your Lord*. You can't remember everything else and forget your Lord.

وَقُلْ عَسَىٰٓ أَن يَهْدِيَنِ رَبِّى لِأَقْرَبَ مِنْ هَٰذَا رَشَدًا

And say, "I hope that my Lord will guide me ever closer (even) than this to the right road"
(Holy Qur'an 18:24)

We said before that the Knowers of Allah are in a state of forgetfulness with regards to the creations, not with regard to the Creator. So, Allah says to us that if we want to do something, we should say *insha'Allah* and this puts you on the right track.

Question 39 – What People are Looking For

People all seem to be searching for something, even though they voice it differently. Is there one thing that everyone is looking for?

There are those who seek God and they know what they are seeking and there are those who seek God and they do not know what they are seeking. Every human being is wired to seek God. This does not mean that He is far away, though. In fact, He is so close to us, and He tells us in His last revelation to mankind, The Holy Qur'an:

وَنَحْنُ أَقْرَبُ إِلَيْهِ مِنْ حَبْلِ ٱلْوَرِيدِ

We are closer to you than your jugular vein

(Holy Qur'an 50:16)

We always seem to be looking outside of our own selves when we look for God, when in reality the whole program is internal. As the Holy Prophet Jesus عَلَيْهِ ٱلسَّلَامُ said, "The kingdom of God is within you." And Allah says in the Holy Qur'an:

وَفِيٓ أَنفُسِكُمۡۚ أَفَلَا تُبۡصِرُونَ

Just as [there are signs thereof] within your own selves: can you not, then, see?

(Holy Qur'an 51:21)

And Allah says in a Holy Saying, "Neither My heavens nor My Earth can contain Me, but the heart of My believing slave contains Me." The (spiritual) human heart – that is where God is.

We said earlier that when one bears witness there is no God but One God and Muhammad is the Messenger of God, this statement is only required from a person once in their lifetime. But the realisation of *La ilaha il Allah*, "There is no God but One God," this must be worked on throughout our life. Every day in our life we have to remember that and we have to bring the realisation. The more we have the realisation of this phrase, the more tranquil and peaceful we become. If we think that the world owes us something, that certain things have to be given to us, or that we have rights over this or that – this is called lack of *adab* with Allah. This means that you have a lack of etiquette and proper manners with God. God wants us to understand that He is the Owner of all things and that He is the Master of all things. Remember that this is for our own benefit as Allah does not need us to acknowledge anything about His Sovereignty.

When you realise that something is not yours, you don't worry too much about parting with it and when you think about it, as Imam al-Ghazali said, "this life is like travelling on a boat." The boat stops at a beautiful island and some of the passengers disembark and walk about. They find many wonderful things there: jewels, fruits, and all kinds of magical things. Some of them look at the island and say, "there are many wonderful things here, but this is not my place." So, they take what is necessary and return to the boat. Some of the people thought it was very nice on the island, decided to stay, and began making plans to build their houses and settle there. The ones who came first got a better place on the island, but when darkness came all the other wonderful things there came out from their places as well. Tigers, snakes, and many other predators came out and destroyed all who stayed behind.

It is the same in the spiritual journey. If you are prepared, you could have a better place, higher knowledge and greater illumination. But if one abandons the ship and stays behind, then they will suffer and perhaps lose everything that they gained on the journey.

This life is like sitting in someone's house as a guest. The host passes a beautiful tray to the guests full of beautiful things for them to see. He says to them, "you may each take something as a souvenir," so each guest in turn chooses something and passes the tray to the next guest. Until it reaches one person who grabs on and doesn't want to let go of it. He says, "this is mine," and he is told, "no, this is not yours, it is meant to move around." The host recommends that we look at it, don't damage anything, handle it with care, take what you need, but you cannot keep hold onto it. This is the problem with this life – we take it, we want to keep it, we want to store it, we damage it, and treat it with disrespect. When it comes time for someone to take it from us, we go screaming and kicking.

People become earth-bound and cause themselves much difficulty. There is a great difference between the one who wants to leave this life for the meeting with their Lord and the one who is earth-bound. For the one who wants to hurry to the meeting, it is as if their coffin almost flies on its own to the burial place. But for the other, it is very heavy and drags those trying to transport it. One is prepared and other is not. Preparation is very necessary.

When one is beginning to seek spiritual knowledge (*ma'rifa*), the first step that one has to take is acknowledgement of Allah and this is the inverse of the treatment in psychology. Psychology begins with the treatment of the organic-self – who is your father, where were you born, what happened in your childhood, and these types of enquiries about the personal experiences in your life. The real teaching tells us that we must begin at the beginning. *Who* built all of this? We must look to the primary cause, or the first cause. This is known as "the

First Cause that does not get affected by desires." As for us, we become affected by our desires every day.

So, when we start to seek the truth, we are seeking the truth about ourselves, about nature, the vegetable kingdom, the animal kingdom, the human kingdom, the angelic kingdom, the Kingdom of the Divine and the Essence of Allah. If you start from the top and work your way down you will be able to understand how Allah manifests Himself in the world.

If we take, for example, our starting point as the Essence of Allah – we are not talking here about the Names of Allah: Allah, Jehovah, God, or any of His Names, but the True Essence – we are not talking here about the Names of God – Allah, Jehovah, or God or any of His Names. When we talk about Essence, really, it is beyond any name or description, because Essence has not opposite. The closest thing to Essence is the Name "Allah." Essence has no limitation. It is in a state of *itlaq* (non-delimitation or infinity). As soon as Essence decides to manifest Itself, then we begin to come to the Name, so we say "God." In our case we speak of the Name "Allah." Allah is the Name which is the manifestation of that Essence. What we have in the world is Essence, Allah, His Names, and His Attributes. Everything that we see with our physical eyes is concerning the Attributes of Allah, how He manifests. You must go beyond the Attributes and Actions to try to find the Names of Allah, or you could say the energy which manifests from Allah to create things.

If we know that the One who created everything is Allah, then the second question we should ask is "How?" We must understand that God does godly things. He doesn't just say "I want to create a human being" and snap His fingers and instantly a human appears. Allah uses what is called the Descent of Being (*tanazzulat*). Creation flows from the higher to the lower. When you say that Allah wanted to create Adam: Adam is the name for all of humankind. Each one of us is "Adam" because each one of us contains all of what is necessary to fulfil the plans of Allah in the universe. Every atom in our bodies is the Universal Man in the making. What this means is that you can become "Godlike" or "Godly."

The Trap of the Weekend Course

If this question of acknowledgement of Allah is not solved within the human, with absolute conviction and belief - not artificial belief, but real, solid belief, then the human cannot develop further to become a human being. This is the foundation that you build your spiritual life on. If the foundation is not strong, then the whole building will collapse. For this reason, the Holy Prophet ﷺ said, "The best that I, and all the Prophets and Messengers before me, brought is *la ilaha il Allah,* 'There is no Allah other than Allah'." This statement is the elimination of all the false gods. A false god is anything that becomes the object and focus of your love. Anything you devote yourself to, then that is your god. If you think you have a wonderful and beautiful car – you put it in the garage and you wash it, and wax it and look after it, don't let anyone touch it - then this means that this is one of the small gods that you worship. If you open your spiritual heart, then you will find that car sitting in there, taking some part of your heart. If you have a beautiful wife, or a beautiful husband, then again, it is the same.

This is not to say that we shouldn't be beautiful or have beautiful things. It is actually the object of life to surround ourselves with beauty because Allah says in a Holy Saying, "Allah is beautiful and He loves beauty." Having beautiful things in life is a part of our spiritual inheritance – it only becomes a problem when the focus is on that object and it becomes the end-in-itself, rather than a means to draw closer to Allah. We cannot see real beauty because we are veiled. We don't operate from a godly point of view, but from the ego-self or the animal-self point of view. What the animal-self likes is ease and comfort. Anything that could exert a little bit of difficulty on her is not acceptable to her.

This is why you find that many people have wonderful experiences when they take a weekend course. You know, you go somewhere, pay a sum of money, really to have your ego stroked and pampered. You earn a certificate in some form of higher knowledge and think that you are really gifted. This makes the ego very happy, but really does nothing towards overcoming and controlling it. Imagine, gaining higher knowledge in a weekend – become a Master in just two days! It took the Prophets 40 or 50 years to gain knowledge. It took Prophet Noah عليه السلام 1000 years to have knowledge of Allah, yet *we* could do it in a weekend. This is illusion. Most people don't want to disturb or have a fight with the ego-self and what happens is the majority of these courses give the ego just what it wants. They caress him, tell him how wonderful he is, and, of course, the weekend is a success and everyone leaves smiling and happy and full of self-love. All of this becomes a trap – *especially* when you get a certificate. This is real proof for someone that they have gotten somewhere. This is a problem in our society – you can look in the newspapers and find all kinds of things.

Many years ago, there was an advertisement for a course in "How to find enlightenment without God." This is like you are saying "Fly without wings." It is impossible to reach anywhere without achieving the first aim, which is an acknowledgement of Allah. Then you could start from the ABC's and gain knowledge slowly to reach that which you already have an innate knowledge of. The realisation of this teaching is "*la ilaha il Allah*." One has to understand that Allah is not in need of anyone to confirm His Unity.

He has already confirmed His Unity to Himself. In the Holy Qur'an, He says:

شَهِدَ ٱللَّهُ أَنَّهُۥ لَآ إِلَـٰهَ إِلَّا هُوَ

Allah bears witness that there is no god but He

(Holy Qur'an 3:18)

And He recommended that we achieve realisation of this: There is no god but One God, There is no Truth but One Truth, There is no Reality but One Reality.

You will find that this is exactly opposite to what the lower-self (*nafs*) wants. The lower-self wants to be a god all by itself. It does not want any higher form of authority, but wants to be the only authority. This is why the lower-self is also known as the "animal-self," with the difference between us and the animal being that that there is an intellect attached to us, and that intellect is the higher-self. With the activation and development of the animal-self, its owner may become a higher human in a state of "being," progressing from being just an ordinary human to a real human being – who is capable of witnessing

Allah. There is no other creation in the world that has the capacity for witnessing Allah. This is what all the teachings, all the revelations, and all the methods which have been given to us through the ages, right up to the final and complete message of the last Prophet, the Holy Prophet Muhammad ﷺ, have been for – to show the human how to have realisation of the formula *la ilaha il Allah,* "There is no god but one God."

This formula is used for meditation, and it is used when a child is born. One of the first things a child hears is this formula whispered into his ear. The first thing that is imprinted on the hard drive of the human is "*la ilaha il Allah.*" The last thing, when someone is dying, this formula is whispered in his ear as well, to remind him. By this time, between his arrival and his departure, he should have accumulated enough knowledge and experience to have achieved unity within himself. You use the unity of "*la ilaha il Allah*" to unify yourself. As we said before, Allah does not have any need for us to confirm His Unity, but the problem of unity is within ourselves. This formula is like the glue which could put us back together. Then when you say “I am,” you are. There is no more division within the self, only unity.

So, you think, and what you think, you say, and what you say, you do, and what you do brings benefit to yourself, to those around you, and to all of the creations. This is the unity of the self. You cannot think things that you would not say as they are regarded as defects. You don’t say what you cannot do, because this would be a breakdown of the self and this is why one has to slowly start to practice.

In the old days people didn’t used to talk much. People would say a few words at most. I remember I watched a film some years ago. The man driving was mapping the desert of North Africa and the woman who accompanied him was talking, and talking, and talking the whole way. He said to her, “Once I travelled with a guide in the desert looking for a town. We started in the morning and he didn’t say anything the whole journey other than to point his finger when we had arrived and say ‘Tofa’. Now that was a good day.”

People today just talk, they exaggerate, stretch the truth and say things that don't mean anything and don't have any value. The Holy Prophet ﷺ said, "From the perfection of one's belief is to leave that which does not concern you" (*Jami' al-Tirmidhi*).

Knowledge and Actions

Now we know everything, but yet, we know nothing. We know who won the latest sports games, but we don't know anything about ourselves. It's a form of catastrophe. Do we think that when we stand before Allah, He is going to ask us who won the World Cup or the score of the latest football match? No, of course not. He will ask us certain important questions: Did you recognise Me in My creation? Did you recognise My manifestations? Did you pray to be near to Me? Did you have enough love in your heart to spread My Goodness to humanity? These are the type of questions He will ask, whether we performed the actions that He recommended through His Prophets and Messengers. He will ask us Godly questions. I don't think He will be asking us about the GST, although He may question the politicians about that one. Everyone has certain responsibilities for themselves, their families, and the community at large, and everyone will be questioned about their own roles.

Allah says, "I did not create you for sport." He created us for a purpose. So, after finding and knowing about Allah, it is then our duty to take the necessary steps to travel back to the Source. This is the aim of life itself. Perhaps one may think that this means that they have to leave everything in order to return. This is not the case, as everything is part of returning back to Allah. This is because everything that we see is spiritual, though it may have a material face. It is our duty, actually, to unmask all of the material faces and find the spiritual faces behind them. Then, even drinking a cup of coffee becomes spiritual. Walking in the street becomes spiritual. Sitting on the bus becomes spiritual. If you are sitting there and you see someone who needs the seat more than you do, then the compassion in your heart gets activated, you stand up, and give it to them. Your activities become spiritual. Whether you remove something out of the way so people don't trip on it, or pick up a piece of bread and place it where the birds can eat it, these are all spiritual actions within your daily life.

If you don't respect these things, these things will leave you. When a person is on his death bed, food and water come to him and they say "Come, we are here, eat and drink," but he will not be able to eat or drink because he now belongs to another realm. And then the Angel who oversees his food and drink will come to him and say, "I have looked everywhere in the worlds, but there is not even one grain left for you. All of your physical provision is gone." His "book" in this life as we know it is finished and the door is open to another life – the spiritual. His life has become inside out. When he was here, his body is outward and the spirit is inward and there, the spirit is outward and the body will be inward. You will not need the body there in the sense that we do here. The interpretation of the dream you have lived in this realm and the actions that you have performed will become manifest in the next realm.

One does need to prepare, and this is not really difficult. It's like having a Master Key. When you have Allah, you can unlock everything and spiritualise everything. If you don't have Allah, you will be in difficulties. When you find Him, you begin to understand that you don't need to be recognised for your good actions. You find that whatever you do, you don't want to speak of it but want to keep it a secret between yourself and the Merciful. Each time you do this, you will find that the doors of the heart will open, the eye of the heart will open, and you will begin to see the Truth.

As we said before, the business of the eye of the heart is for us to see Allah and for Allah to see us. All of these activities that we do are so that the window or the eye of the heart will be opened.

May Allah guide us and make us successful, *insha'Allah*.

بسم الله الرحمن الرحيم

Question 40 – The Saints of Allah

Who are the Saints of Allah?

There are 4,000 *walis* (friends of God) who are not known to the world. They do not know one another, nor are they conscious of their exalted position. They ever remain veiled from the world, as well as from themselves.

There are 300 *akhyar* (the Charitable or the Benevolent) who solve the difficulties of the world and keep the gate of the Divine Sanctuary. There are 40 *abdal* (the Substitutes); 17 *abrar* (the Liberated); 5 *nujaba* (the Pure); 4 *awtad* (the Pegs or Pillars); 3 *nuqaba* (the Watchers); 1 *qutub* (the Pole), also called *ghawth* (the Help), the "Redresser of Grievances." All these know one another and are interdependent for the discharge of their respective duties.

According to another authority (*Majma-us-Saerin*) there are 356 *walis* ever working in the world. When one of them retires, another takes his place, so that there is never any diminution in the number 356. They are made up of 300 + 40 + 7 + 5 + 3 + 1. The one is the *qutub* of the world, the preservation of which is due to his holy existence. If he retired without another to take his place, the world would fall to pieces. When the *qutub* retires, one of the three takes His place; one of the five fills up the gap in the three, one of the seven fills up the gap in the five, one of the forty fills up the gap in the seven, one of the three hundred fills up the gap in the forty, and a man is posted to the vacancy in the rank of the three hundred - so that 356 continue working in the world, and every spot is blessed by their auspicious feet. Their outer life is similar to ordinary people, so the latter cannot know them. Inwardly, they are united with God. Love, friendship, and the mysteries have to do with the *within*, not with the *without*. They (the *walis*) are too strong to be hindered by earth, water, fire, air, plains, and hills. Being in the East they can see and hear men in the West. They can instantly go from the East to the West, come from the West to the East, go to and come back from *al-'arsh* (the Divine Throne). Theirs are many superhuman powers of like nature.

Question 41 – *Adab al-Zawiyya* - The Etiquette and Proper Behaviour of Attending the Sufi Centre

What is the proper etiquette of attending the Sufi Centre?

وَإِذَا جَآءَكَ ٱلَّذِينَ يُؤْمِنُونَ بِـَٔايَـٰتِنَا فَقُلْ سَلَـٰمٌ عَلَيْكُمْ
كَتَبَ رَبُّكُمْ عَلَىٰ نَفْسِهِ ٱلرَّحْمَةَ أَنَّهُۥ مَنْ عَمِلَ مِنكُمْ
سُوٓءًۢا بِجَهَـٰلَةٍ ثُمَّ تَابَ مِنۢ بَعْدِهِۦ وَأَصْلَحَ فَأَنَّهُۥ
غَفُورٌ رَّحِيمٌ

When those come to you who believe in Our signs, say "Peace be upon you, your Sustainer has written upon himself Mercy. If any of you did evil in ignorance of the truth, and then repents and mends his conduct, surely, He is oft forgiving, Most Merciful"

(Holy Qur'an 6:54)

إِنَّمَا ٱلْمُؤْمِنُونَ ٱلَّذِينَ إِذَا ذُكِرَ ٱللَّهُ وَجِلَتْ قُلُوبُهُمْ وَإِذَا
تُلِيَتْ عَلَيْهِمْ ءَايَٰتُهُۥ زَادَتْهُمْ إِيمَٰنًا وَعَلَىٰ رَبِّهِمْ يَتَوَكَّلُونَ
ٱلَّذِينَ يُقِيمُونَ ٱلصَّلَوٰةَ وَمِمَّا رَزَقْنَٰهُمْ يُنفِقُونَ
أُوْلَٰٓئِكَ هُمُ ٱلْمُؤْمِنُونَ حَقًّا لَّهُمْ دَرَجَٰتٌ عِندَ رَبِّهِمْ
وَمَغْفِرَةٌ وَرِزْقٌ كَرِيمٌ

Believers are only they whose hearts tremble with awe whenever Allah is mentioned, and whose faith is strengthened whenever His messages are conveyed unto them, and who in their Sustainer place their trust - those who are constant in prayer and spend on others out of what We provide for them as sustenance; it is they, they who are truly believers! Theirs shall be great dignity in their Sustainer's sight, and forgiveness of sins, and a most excellent sustenance.

(Holy Qur'an 8:2-4)

ظَهَرَ ٱلْفَسَادُ فِى ٱلْبَرِّ وَٱلْبَحْرِ بِمَا كَسَبَتْ أَيْدِى ٱلنَّاسِ
لِيُذِيقَهُم بَعْضَ ٱلَّذِى عَمِلُوا۟ لَعَلَّهُمْ يَرْجِعُونَ

Corruption has appeared on land and in the sea as an outcome of what men's hands have wrought: and so He will let them taste [the evil of] some of their doings, so that they might return [to the right path]
(Holy Qur'an 30:41)

The Holy Prophet ﷺ said, "*Al-Deen al-Mu'amala* (The religion is good actions)."

For everything in life there is a code of conduct, certain behaviour which is acceptable and desirable for each situation. It is common sense we behave in our homes with our families in a different way than when we are with our friends, in our working environment, and other situations. The guidelines are different in every situation, but the difference is in degree, not in kind, as good manners are always desirable.

Certain qualities are natural to some people and for others, they need to work to obtain such qualities. If the qualities that we have are truthfulness, sincerity, kindness, concern for others, honesty, and the like, we earn the respect of those around us as everyone loves such qualities and respect the individuals who have them. But, as I said, for others, they will need to work to make these qualities part of their selves. We could fill pages, or even books, writing on the subject of the negative and positive qualities of the human being and the manners of conduct in every field of life. However, that would take us too far from our purpose of writing this *nasihah* (sincere advice) for the seeker of truth (*salik*) and specifically for anyone who is a visitor to the Centre or is part of the Islamic Sufi Order.

The purpose of establishing a Sufi Centre is to know Allah. This place is for those who desire and wish with their entire being to be nearer to the Source of Life, Knowledge, and Love.

First, we would like to explain what the Sufi Centre is and what it takes to establish and to maintain such a place.

We all need the means to buy, to sell, to do business; and we work so that we can maintain our lives. The same principle applies to spiritual places. The help of the Divine Generosity is there, but human beings who have a connection with a Sufi Centre also have the responsibility for establishing it, maintaining it, and looking after the Centre and especially the teaching they are given, for this is the purpose of establishing such a place.

What we mean by "looking after the teaching" is that you are each individually responsible to complete and maintain your own spiritual practices which include your five daily prayers, reading of the Holy Qur'an, following the Sunnah of the Holy Prophet ﷺ, and the completing of the practices which have been designated by the Islamic Sufi Order to which you belong.

When we look at the world today and we see programs on television, the mountains are there, the seas are there, rivers are there, animals are there, and all different kinds of cities and countries. Airplanes, trains, cars, motorcycles, and bicycles are all there on the screen. From the physical point of view, many things do not seem to have changed, but upon closer examination and investigation, we live in this new millennium with a completely different brain set and complex mental attitudes and behaviour that is totally off the chart from what used to be considered acceptable.

As we have said before in many of the things we have written - humanity has evolved dramatically in the technological realm. We are technologically advanced and modernised, but sadly the steps that need to be taken towards being civilised have not been taken. For this reason, all the new technologies available to humanity such as instant communications, internet, video and conference calls, and of course other technological advancements and entertainment options, have given us the illusion that we are intelligent and clever and that we know exactly what we are doing.

We cannot deny the certain degree of benefit for humanity with regards to technology. It has brought a degree of benefit and ease to our lives. But, because of the absence of the moral component, the moral code which enables the human to evolve to become a human being and live in peace with himself, his environment, and with the world in general; we do not have peace or happiness or even a reasonably well-adjusted self. Most people are constantly in a state of strife - inward strife, outward strife, and peace and happiness just do not exist for them. You do not have to take my word for it; just ask the nearest one to you - even if it be a stranger - what they think of the situation of the world today. The answer will be "terrible," or something similar, without any hesitation. People know that humanity has taken a turn for the worse and they are heading towards uncharted territory and an uncertain future. What will it benefit the intelligent individual who has a house full of the latest gadgets and new inventions if he does not have the spiritual awareness and concern for human life to bring happiness to others instead of increasing their misery? This detachment from caring and inner considering is one of our major shortcomings and a disastrous outcome of modernisation.

As the Holy One ﷺ has said, "At the end of the cycle, mankind will live in a state of war and rumours of war."

Day in and day out, we are bombarded with the news of killing, destruction of property, land, cities, and countries, by forces both natural and man-made. Every country is armed to the teeth, or they are trying to arm themselves, for the sake of protection, like the world is going to be invaded by aliens from outer space. The idea of "love thy neighbour" now falls on deaf ears. We sincerely wish that people who are able, or desire, to live in peace will be able to do so. Because of the lack of realisation of true knowledge, real knowing, of the purpose and the aim of our existence on planet earth, peace is elusive to most.

For this reason, a Sufi Centre is one of the real factors in laying foundations for individuals, communities, and, to a certain degree, brings solace and the Divine Pleasure to humanity in general. Such a place will not give benefit to anyone if the people who are directly connected to it, near and far, do not take the spiritual teaching which has been made available for them seriously, use it properly and practice it - practice regularly with sincerity, focus and harmony.

So, we come back to the question – the *adab,* or the manners of the residents and the visitors to such a Holy place. How they should behave so that they could gain the maximum spiritual benefit from the time they spend and to awaken the sleeper within and develop great and powerful *himma* (determination). All the aims we wish to achieve will be ours to receive through the Grace of the Loving and Generous and Merciful Allah.

The Spiritual Centre is established by Allah, for Allah, so that we may achieve the ultimate and the beautiful destination of travel within Allah. *Kun ma'a Allah,* be with Allah. In this time and age we live in, to find a Sufi Centre and to be part of that Centre, in comparison to what has been said earlier, one should consider himself truly lucky, truly successful, and truly blessed. The Divine Hand has pushed you onto the right path, on to the *Sirat al-Mustaqeem* - "the Path of those whom You have favoured and given success to."

It has been said in the eternal language, "He has brought you out of the darkness into the light." This is indeed a

Divine favour and one should be eternally grateful to the Loving and Merciful Allah for bestowing guidance upon us. Anyone who is a part of Islamic Sufism should have a good understanding of why they are connected to such a teaching because this great teaching can fill your heart with knowledge, with realisations, with peace, acceptance, and the true purpose of one's life.

The Holy Prophet ﷺ said, "There is no shyness in spiritual teaching" (*Sahih Bukhari*). This means that if you do not know, you should ask and if you need help, you should seek the appropriate assistance. With the sheer volume of knowledge that is available to us in the 21st century in books, talks, and online resources, there is no reason for anyone to be ignorant of this great teaching. That being said, there is no substitute for a living teacher and the company of like-minded people with the same spiritual aim.

It has been said, "Whoever spends 40 days in the company of a group will become one of them." For this reason, *suhba* (spiritual companionship) is one of the greatest and most blessed situations in life that one could find himself in. We are saying all this again to jog the awareness and to remind ourselves why we go to a Sufi Centre, why do we visit such a place, and how to achieve the maximum benefit from the time spent there.

A Sufi Centre is not a coffee shop, even though coffee is being served.

It is not a restaurant, even though food may be served there.

It is not a place to drop in to use the sanitation facilities, even though these facilities have been made available.

It is a place of learning.

If learning and increasing your knowledge is not your aim, then don't go to the Sufi Centre and spoil the efforts of those who are sincere and genuine in seeking the higher teaching with your negative thoughts and actions.

I hope that by now, the question has arisen in your minds. So, ask yourself, "Why are you here?" And when you have answered this question, then ask, "What should I do when I am here in this place of learning?" I am very glad that you have asked.

Let us start with the inward mechanism that is known as "intention." Traditionally, it has been said that all actions are based on intention. The deeper and more sincere the intentions, the more successful you will become in gaining the greater knowledge. We will put them in sequence to make it clear:

1) When you arrive at the Sufi Centre, you should be in a state of ritual purity – having ablution. If you are not in a state of *wudhu*, immediately upon arrival, greet those who are in the Centre with a proper, respectful greeting and excuse yourself to make ablutions. If you do not know where the facilities are, ask.

2) An Islamic Sufi Centre has similarities to the *masjid* (mosque), a place of worship. In such a sacred place, it is highly recommended to convey your greetings by offering

two cycles (*rakat*) of prayer. This is known as *tahiyyat ul-masjid* - the greeting of the mosque.

3) If prayer is taking place when you arrive, you should quietly join in. Do not say to yourself or others "I have already done this or that at home." You are now on different ground. There is no harm in repetition, but there is spiritual grace and the offering of supplications, and you should not cut yourself off from such activities. Every one of us, at one time or another, have missed or forgotten a prayer so joining in will be of great benefit to you.

4) If teaching is taking place when you arrive, the same etiquettes apply - offer your greetings with proper respect and then join in quietly, finding yourself a place to sit without disturbing the flow of what is happening. Do not ask anyone what you have missed as you will find that, if you stay long enough, the teaching will embrace you and you will have gained the knowledge that you have missed earlier by the *baraka* and Divine Light and the presence of spiritual beings who surround such a gathering. You will have partaken of this beautiful celestial food.

5) If you have brought food to share with your brothers and sisters, you should place it quietly, nicely, and properly on the kitchen bench or other designated place for such items. You should absolutely never bring food just for your own self and eat it by your own self. This is not acceptable and is bad manners of the highest degree. Do not write your name on items of food or drink in the Sufi Centre, whether in the kitchen, the refrigerator, the oven, or microwave, because sharing with others and controlling one's appetites will increase the will power and develop generosity. Eating alone when there are others around or bringing food only for yourself is not allowed. The exception being when you arrive as a meal is being finished, or has already been finished, and you are offered food. In this case, you should accept what is being offered, trying to avoid saying "thank you, I have eaten," "I'm not hungry," "I don't like this," "I don't like that," or "I have never eaten that." All of this is unnecessary and there is no call for it. You are here to learn and the learning begins in the kitchen. In the traditional Sufi Centre, the one who cooks and serves others and slaves over a hot stove for the sake of feeding others is usually the one who was brought to the gathering to make supplication to

the real Giver, the Sustainer, our Beloved Allah. As the Holy One ﷺ has said, "The servant of the group is their leader (*khadim al-qawm amirahum*)" (*Sunan Ibn Majah*). In a nutshell, if you are hungry, eat, if you are full, have a few morsels for the blessing contained within them. Everyone nowadays has a house full of food and a supermarket nearby supplied with the best produce. The food is not the aim, it is a means to an end.

6) If you find yourself alone in the Centre, you must know that you are never alone. As the Holy One ﷺ said, "If you cannot see God, then you must know that He sees you" (*Sunan al-Nasa'i*). So go about your spiritual business, do your prayer, perform your spiritual practices if you have not done so, and then, one of the best things you can do for your spiritual Centre is to keep it clean.

7) It has been said, "Cleanliness is from the illumination of one's belief (*an-natafa min al-iman*)." Cleanliness is part of belief. If there are dishes to be cleaned, then wash them. If there is a table to be wiped, then do so. If vacuuming is required or the sanitation facilities need attention, then

that also is your job. Look and see what needs to be done and do it. Do not come in like a whirlwind and, if there is no one there, have a cup of coffee and move on. If you do this, your footprints will leave an unpleasant residue (*athar*). Be conscious, be respectful, and be aware of where you are, who you are, and to whom this place really belongs. It belongs to the Almighty Allah, the Seer of all things. It is the place of love, a place of kindness, a place of respect, a place to train the ego self to walk behind the heart, not in front of it. That is a Sufi Centre.

8) In the Centre, there is always a spiritual event taking place. There are the daily prayers, the Friday prayer, and the weekly gathering for the Remembrance of Allah. There are marriages taking place and there are guests who come from faraway places for the sole reason of visiting the Sufi Centre. They need to be attended to and looked after with proper respect and hospitality.

9) As a *murid*, regardless of whether you are working or not, there are two things during the week that you should do your utmost to participate in. One is the weekly

gathering of *dhikr* and the second is the Friday prayer. If you are a *murid,* you should never miss these two events. Rearrange your life so you will benefit greatly by participating in such activities. Bend yourself to the teaching, do not try to bend the teaching to yourself or your schedule. If you do not do so, you must question your own sincerity and your motive for connecting yourself with the Sufi teaching.

10) Everyone has family and work to do outside of the Sufi Centre. There are 168 hours in each week. The teaching asks you to sacrifice only a few of these for your own benefit. Four hours on Friday and four hours for the gathering of *dhikr* (remembrance of Allah). If you are not able to make this effort, then you are missing a great part of your celestial and spiritual sustenance. You really need to examine your life and set things straight, because there is something drastically wrong. We have said many times before that being on time or early is one of the good qualities of every Muslim. Those who are consistently late or leaving before the gathering has closed must also seriously question their reasons for being here at all.

11) Etiquette of Proper Dress. Proper dress for men, women, and children who are nearing maturity is an essential part of the teaching. Modesty is a key to spiritual travel. Proper clothing for both men and women includes loose garments which are opaque and do not have any imagery or advertisements printed on them so that they do not disturb others. Head coverings for ladies should cover the head, neck, and shoulders, be opaque, and securely fastened to avoid the need for any adjustment. The same rules apply to any guests that you bring to the Centre. They should be advised beforehand that proper clothing is a requirement of attendance. Do not feel embarrassed by asking them to dress properly. If you bring a guest into the Centre, you are responsible for looking after them. Do not embarrass them or yourself by neglecting this. There are change rooms available for both men and women in the Sufi Centre. Please ensure that when you enter the prayer area, you are already properly dressed. Do not ever use this Sacred Space as a change room.

12) Children in the Sufi Centre. Sufi communities in general are very loving, kind, and caring people. Having children in

the Sufi Centre is always a welcome occasion so that they can see and learn from their encounters with the elders of the community. Anyone who brings children has the responsibility of looking after them and to make sure that they do not cause any damage or break anything or make a racket while they are there. Children are always welcome, but there are also responsibilities towards them and the Centre. If we are in prayer, or in the circle of *dhikr,* or in study, you should make sure that they are safe and looked after and that the noise is kept to a minimum and does not become a disturbance to the gathering. It is good for them to be encouraged to participate in the prayer and *dhikr*.

13) At the Centre, there is order. In the Sufi teaching in general there is order, so one must ask permission for certain things. There is the Shaykh or the *Murshid* of the *zawiyya* and there may also be a *Khalifah,* a *Muqaddam,* a *Wasi,* or one of the elders who has been appointed to look after things. These people should be asked about any concerns or questions that you may have and an answer should not be expected or demanded immediately. Go through the proper channels and it will be better for you.

If you need help, it is very wise and a good decision to ask for it. As we have said earlier, if you do not know, ask.

14) Very Good Advice: The Holy One ﷺ said, "When a believer speaks, he tells the truth, when he promises, he keeps his promise and if he is entrusted with something, he keeps his trust." This indeed is beautiful and wonderful advice to implement not just in the Centre, but in our everyday lives. In the Sufi Centre, a library of books and audio visual material is available for study within the Centre, so please make good use of them, but make sure that, as with everything, when you leave, leave things in as good or better condition than when you arrived.

15) We live in this world and we have responsibilities and duties in this realm. It would be nice if we could shut them off, but the truth is that we cannot shut them off totally from our lives while we are in the Centre. However, it will be of great benefit to you if you do not cloud your thoughts and your focus with talk of useless and worldly topics. If you have the honour of sitting in the presence of the Shaykh, pay close attention to what is

being said, take notes and use those notes to study, follow up on clues that you are given, and acquire further knowledge. At no time should *murids* be engaging in conversation in the presence of the *Murshid* unless they are directly asked to speak. When sitting with the Shaykh or *Murshid*, your *tasbih* should be put away. Any personal spiritual work should be done at a time when you are not sitting in the presence of the Shaykh.

16) We said earlier the Sufi Centre is similar to the *masjid* or mosque in that it is a place of worship, prayer, and the Remembrance of God. It is a sacred space and should be treated as such. Look after your Centre and your Centre will look after you.

17) Even billionaires worry about money. The more that we are disconnected from the Beloved Allah, the more these worries increase, regardless of whether we have or we have not. The Holy Prophet ﷺ recommended that we should respect his Companions and learn the teaching from them, because they are the inheritors of knowledge. As Sayyidina 'Umar ibn al-Khattab ؓ, the second

successor to the Holy Prophet ﷺ said, "The sky does not rain gold or silver," and the Holy Prophet ﷺ has said that there will come a time for humanity that no one will be able to live without money and every one of us knows this quite well. Your contributions towards the running of the Sufi Centre are a duty, but they also contain tremendous spiritual blessing. You must remember that whatever contribution you make in the Centre will be of great benefit to you and will put spiritual blessing into your life and success in whatever you do. So, in reality, you are not giving, you are receiving. Never see yourself as being short, but that you are increasing in tremendous spiritual deeds and illuminations of your heart.

18) Last, but not least, you should always speak highly of your place of learning with honour, dignity, and respect. You have been given the opportunity today to be in the Centre. In the future there will be others who will come after you to learn and to drink from the Celestial and Divine Water of Life. You should know that Allah is the First and the Last. He is the Inward, He is the Outward and He encompasses all things.

19) The foundation of the Centre is *Ashadu an la ilaha il Allah, wa ashadu anna Muhammadan 'abduhu wa rasuluhu* and stay on the Straight Path.

All the fragrant and beautiful salutations and peace be upon the one who has been sent as a Mercy to all of the creations and among his family and his wives, the mothers of the believers, and his companions until the Day of Judgement. And the last of our supplications is *Alhamdulillahi Rabbil 'Alamein*. All Praise belongs to Allah, the Lord of the Universe.

The Hymn of the Pearl

When I was a little child,
and dwelling in my kingdom,
in my father's house,
and was content with the wealth and the
luxuries of my nourishers,
from the East, our home,
my parents equipped me (and) sent me forth;
and of the wealth of our treasury
they took abundantly, (and) tied up for me a load
large and (yet) light, which I myself could carry,
gold of Beth-Ellaya,
and silver of Gazak the great,
and rubies of India,
and agates from Beth-Kashan,
and they furnished me with the adamant,
which can crush iron.
And they took off from me the glittering robe,
which in their affection they made for me,

and the purple mantle,
which was measured (and) woven to my stature.
And they made a compact with me,
and wrote it in my heart, that it might not be forgotten:
"If thou goest down into Egypt,
and bringest the one pearl,
which is in the midst of the sea
around the loud-breathing serpent,
thou shalt put on thy glittering robe
and thy mantle, with which (thou art) contented,
and with thy brother, who is next to us in authority,
thou shalt be heir in our kingdom."
I quitted the East (and) went down,
there being two guardians,
for the way was dangerous and difficult,
and I was very young to travel it.
I passed through the borders of Maishan,
the meeting-place of the merchants of the East,
and I reached the land of Babel,
and I entered the walls of Sarbug.
I went down into Egypt,
and my companions parted from me.

I went straight to the serpent,
I dwelt in his abode,
(waiting) till he should lumber and sleep,
and I could take my pearl from him.
And when I was single and alone
(and) became strange to my family,
one of my race, a free-born man,
and Oriental, I saw there,
a youth fair and loveable,
the son of oil-sellers;
and he came and attached himself to me,
and I made him my intimate friend,
and associate with whom I shared my merchandise.
I warned him against the Egyptians,
and against consorting with the unclean;
And I dressed in their dress,
that they might not hold me in abhorrence,
because I was come from abroad in order to take the pearl,
and arouse the serpent against me.
But in some way other or another
they found out that I was not their countryman,
and they dealt with me treacherously,

and gave their food to eat.
I forget that I was a son of kings,
and I served their king;
and I forgot the pearl,
for which my parents had sent me,
and because of the burden of their oppressions
I lay in a deep sleep.
But all these things that befell me
my parents perceived, and were grieved for me;
and proclamation was made in our kingdom,
that everyone should come to our gate,
kings and princes of Parthia,
and all the nobles of the East.
And they wove a plan on my behalf,
that I might not be left in Egypt;
and they wrote to me a letter,
and every noble signed his name to it:
"From thy father, the king of kings,
and thy mother, the mistress of the East,
and from thy brother, our second (in authority),
to thee our son, who art in Egypt, greeting!
Call to mind that thou art a son of kings!

See the slavery, whom thou servest!
Remember the pearl,
for which thou was sent to Egypt!
Think of thy robe,
and remember thy splendid mantle,
which thou shalt wear and (with which) thou shalt be adorned,
when thy name hath been read out in the list of the valiant,
and thy brother, our viceroy,
thou shalt be in our kingdom."
My letter is a letter,
which the king sealed with his own right hand,
(to keep it) from the wicked ones, the children of Babel,
and from the savage demons of Sarbug.
It flew in the likeness of an eagle,
the king of all birds;
it flew and alight beside me,
and became all speech.
At its voice and the sound of its rustling,
I started and arose from my sleep.
I took it up and kissed it,

and I began (and) read it;
and according to what was traced on my heart
were the words of my letter.
I remembered that I was a son of royal parents,
and my noble birth asserted itself.
I remembered the pearl,
for which I had been sent to Egypt,
and I began to charm him,
the terrible loud breathing serpent.
I hushed him asleep and lulled him into slumber,
for my father's name I named over him,
and the name of our second (in power),
and the name of my mother, the Queen of the East.
And I snatched away the pearl,
and turned to go back to my father's house.
And their filthy and unclean dress I stripped off,
and left it in their country;
and I took my way straight to come
to the light of our home in the East.
And my letter, my awakener,
I found before me on the road;
and as with its voice it had awakened me,

(so) too with its light it was leading me.
It, that dwelt in the palace,
gave light before me with its form,
and with its voice and its guidance
it also encouraged me to speed,
and with its love it drew me on.
I went forth (and) passed by Sarbug;
I left Babel on my left hand;
and I came to the great Maisan,
to the haven of merchants,
which sitteth on the shore of the sea.
And my bright robe, which I had stripped off,
and the mantle that was wrapped with it,
Down from the heights of Hyrcania, my parents had sent thither
by the hand of their treasures,
who in their truth could be trusted therewith.
And because I remembered not its fashion,
for in my childhood I had left it in my father's house,
on a sudden, when I received it,
the garment seemed to me to become like a mirror of myself.

I saw it all in all,
and I too received all in it,
for we were two in distinction
and yet gain one in one likeness.
And the treasurers too,
who brought it to me, I saw in like manner
to be two (and yet) one likeness,
for one sign of the king was written on them (both),
of the hands of him who restored to me through them
my trust and my wealth,
my decorated robe, which
was adorned with glorious colours,
with gold and beryls
and rubies and agates
and sardonyxes, varied in colour.
And it was skilfully worked in its home on high,
and with diamond clasps
were all its seams fastened;
and the image of the king of kings
was embroidered and depicted in full all over it,
and like the stone of the sapphire too
its hues were varied.

And I saw also that all over it
the instincts of knowledge were working,
and I saw too that it was preparing to speak.
I heard the sound of its tones,
which it uttered with its voice, (saying):
"I am the active in deeds,
whom they reared for him before my father;
and I perceived myself,
that my stature grew according to his labours."
And in its kingly movements
it poured itself entirely over me,
and on the hand of its givers
it hastened that I might take it.
And love urged me to run
to meet it and receive it;
and I stretched forth and took it.
With the beauty of its colours I adorned myself,
and I wrapped myself wholly in my mantle
of brilliant hues.
I clothed myself with it, and went up to the gate
of salutation and prostration;
I bowed my head and worshipped the majesty

of my father who sent me,
for I had done his commandments, and he too had done
what he promised,
and the gate of his house,
I mingled with his princes,
for he rejoiced in me and received me,
and I was with him in his kingdom,
and with the voice of love
all his servants praised him.
He had promised that with him
to the Court of the King of Kings I should speed,
and with my offering and my pearl
with him should present myself to our king.

Glossary

abdal: Changed Ones. Within the Sufi hierarchy there are seven (or forty) men (or women) called "the changed ones."

'abid: Worshipper.

abrar: The Liberated. Within the Sufi hierarchy there are seventeen who are called "the Liberated."

adab: Spiritual courtesy. It is spiritual courtesy and gracious behaviour of the Path and perfect refinement of words and deeds. *Adab* is giving each thing and each moment its proper due. The science of the higher teaching is based upon *adab,* which encompasses all human life. It extends from right behaviour with regard to the Sacred Law (*shari'ah*), right behaviour with one's fellow travellers, proper conduct towards the teaching and one's teacher, and reaches to unceasing spiritual courtesy to Allah Himself. The proper courtesy towards the Law is to stay within its boundaries. The proper conduct with regards to good actions is to complete the action and disconnect from it. *Adab* with regard to the Real is knowing what belongs to oneself and what belongs to Allah. Each moment and each situation has its own *adab*. It has been said that the higher teaching is all *adab* and the greater your understanding and implementation of proper conduct is, the higher you are in the teaching.

akhyar: The Good. Within the Sufi hierarchy there are three hundred who are called "the Good."

'arif: Knower. He is the complete and perfect man. The *'arif* has been given Divine Knowledge (*ma'rifa*), and *ma'rifa* is a light which Allah casts into the heart of whomsoever He Wills. All is a gift from Allah. The knower is the aware one, the wise one. He has penetrated the mystery of the paradoxical relationship between the One and the Many, between Allah and His creation. His Lord causes the knower to witness his own self, so that spiritual states are manifested to him. The knower who is also a lover is the most perfect of human beings.

al-asaas: The Foundation. A house will not stand firm without a solid foundation. Starting from the foundation the murid methodically reconstructs his entire being. The building process starts with his first spiritual practices (*awrad*). If these are approached and fulfilled with sincerity, need, and love then his foundation (*asaas*) will be solid. Ultimately the foundation of everything is Allah.

al-'Aleem: The Knower. One of the Beautiful Names of Allah.

'alim: Knower. The one who knows. This term derives from the word "knowledge" (*'ilm*). Usually it refers to the exoteric scholars, though sometimes *'aleem* is used in reference to "those who know Allah." The "one who knows" is the one whom Allah causes to witness his godhead (*uluhiyyah*) and His Essence. No states manifest to him, knowledge is his condition.

al-'arsh: The Divine throne. Allah, Who is without place, created a heaven called "the Throne" where He could "sit" in order for man to supplicate and seek his needs from Allah. This Throne upon which Allah "sits" is the seat of those Divine Names that are bound to a place. The Divine Word which descends from Allah contains the Sacred Law within which is all knowledge. The "place" of Unity of the Word is His Throne (*al-'arsh*). Beneath the Throne is His Footstool where the Word becomes differentiated into rulings or judgements and reports. Although the earth and the heaven do not contain Allah, the heart of His slave does contain Allah. Such a heart is *al-'arsh*. It is the heart of the Lover of Allah and around it the spiritual-realities circle. *al-'arsh* is the universal-manifestation taken in its total-unfolding. The greatest heart is that of the Holy Prophet Muhammad ﷺ. All knowledge and love are an overflowing from his heart.

'ashiq: Lover. The *'ashiq* is the one who searches for Allah with intense yearning and longing, never allowing himself rest in his pursuit of the Beloved. The perfect lover of Allah loves Allah in every Self-disclosure.

athar: Traces. Remainders or traces or vestiges or effects. The effects of the Divine Names are the phenomena of the cosmos. That is, the things and the forms and the entities which manifest the Names are the effects. When the inner-eye is opened the seer sees the effects, and he sees the Names and realities of these effects and therefore he sees them as a manifestation of the Essence Itself.

awra: The area of the body that should not be exposed to view is known as the *awra*. For women, this includes everything but the hands and face, for men, it is the area between the navel and the knees. Uncovering the *awra* at any time during prayer invalidates the prayer.

awrad: Spiritual Work. This is the spiritual work undertaken by the *murid* with the direct permission of his Murshid. The *awrad* consists of units of *dhikr*, in the form of repetition of Divine Names, Qur'anic verses, and sacred litanies. Within *tariqa* it is the actual doing of the *awrad* which results in a gradual and beautiful inner transformation. However, the degree of spiritual transformation depends, firstly and ultimately, upon the Grace of Allah, and, secondly, upon the purity of intention and sincerity of the *murid*. The Murshid distributes the *awrad*, but it is the *murid* who is required to do the *awrad*.

awtad: The Pegs or Pillars. Within the Sufi hierarchy there are four who are called "the Pillars."

'ayn al-yaqin: The Eye of Certainty. In the triad of the Knowledge of Certainty, the Eye of Certainty, and the Truth of Certainty, the Eye of Certainty could be likened to actually seeing the light of the flames of a fire, after having merely heard a description of that fire. This is the stage of knowledge before being consumed by the flames themselves (Truth of Certainty). The Eye of Certainty is the inner eye or insight. The opening of this "eye" is a miracle and a mystery and it only comes about through the Mercy of the All Merciful. It is Allah's gift to His slave through His Infinite Grace. The seven levels of knowledge through which the traveller must pass on his journey of return to the Source are Surrender, Belief, Perfection, Knowledge of Certainty, Eye of Certainty, Truth of Certainty, and unconditional surrender with Knowledge.

baqa': Abiding in Allah. Subsistence with Allah for perpetuity. After the stage of annihilation in Allah, Allah either keeps His slave in this station of stations or He sends him back to the world to perfect the still imperfect ones. Abiding is the slave's return to humanity in the robes of honour. Now he sees Allah established in everything and at all times. *Baqa'* corresponds to the third and final stage of self-annihilation. This is the condition of the slave and the friend.

baraka: Spiritual Energy. It is a subtle spiritual energy which flows through everything, though strongest within the human. The more purified the human becomes, the greater the flow of *baraka*. Overpowering *baraka* can be experienced in sacred places, in sacred art, and in sanctified people, all of which are theophanies, revealing and manifesting the Divinity – here on earth.

bay'ah: Pledge of Initiation. The pledge or rite of initiation into a Sufi *tariqa*. This pledge, which in truth is a pledge between Allah and His slave, eternally bonds together the Murshid and his *murid*. Within the *bay'ah* there is a sacred moment in which the spiritual energy of the spiritual chain is transmitted from the Murshid to the *murid*. This enables the *murid* to travel in safety under Divine Protection and with Divine Aid.

bushra: Good News. Good news and glad tidings which may be heralded within dreams and visions or may arrive in the heart while under the powerful influence of a spiritual state (*hal*).

deen: Life Transaction. The word *deen* indicates the life transaction between Allah and Man. It is not merely religion in the constricted and limited sense, which the word has assumed in these times. This life transaction is between Allah and man, between the Creator and the created, the Limitless and the limited, the One and the many. Life transaction includes every facet, every aspect of life – from the smallest detail to the greatest action. Every moment of a man's life should be impregnated with the awareness of Allah – life is meaningless and futile without such an awareness. Islam, the Perfect and Final Revelation, is the Straight Path to this awareness of the Source. The higher teaching is the Living Heart of Islam – the Heart from which flows the life-giving nourishment to every soul in the manifested world.

dhikr: Remembrance. Remembrance, invocation, or glorification of Allah, through the repetition of one of His Names or a phrase to His Glory. True *dhikr* is a spiritual state in which the one who remembers (*dhakir*) concentrates all his physical and spiritual powers upon Allah so that his entire being may be united with the Absolute. It is the fundamental practice of the Sufi path and may be undertaken in solitude or in gatherings. Specific breathing patterns are central to the effectiveness of the *dhikr*.

dua': Supplication. *Du'a* is the private and personal supplication of the slave to his Lord. "Your Lord hath said, 'Call upon Me and I will answer you." (Holy Qur'an 2:260). "Call upon Allah, or call upon *Rahman*, by whatever name ye call upon Him (it is well), for to Him belong the Most Beautiful Names" (Holy Qur'an 17:110). This personal form of prayer gives to the worshipper the opportunity to pour out his heart, expressing his longings, his fears, and his intense need of his Lord. In doing so man can rid himself of accumulated poisons and emotional debris which block the celestial channel between himself and Allah Almighty. Sitting, with head bowed and palms upturned in an attitude of readiness to receive the *baraka* from above, man may become a symbol, not only of spiritual poverty but also one of supreme trust.

fada'il: Kindness.

fana': Annihilation. Self-annihilation or self-effacement or dissolution or passing away from self. Through being joined to Allah, the Real, man is annihilated from himself. The "limited existence" of the traveller is overpowered by the "absolute existence" of Allah so the traveller becomes unaware of his own self and the creation. *Fana'* is the last stage on the ascent to Allah. When travelling to the Source, the seeker passes through different levels of *fana'*, each of which brings him closer to his Goal. There are hundreds, even thousands, of *fana's*. Every time a form of ignorance is removed to be replaced by knowledge, the *murid* has experienced *fana'*. He has tasted the annihilation of an ignorance. Every moment of existence is in fact a moment which is pregnant with its own particular knowledge. So, for the aware one, each moment can be a *fana'*. However, within the higher teaching of *tasawwuf* there are three major types of *fana'* through which the *murid* must travel if he is to reach the Absolute. These are Annihilation in the *Murshid*/Spiritual Guide, Annihilation in the Messenger, and Annihilation in Allah.

fikr: Reflection. Reflection or the power of thought and cogitation. It is the ability to put together the details accumulated by the senses and acquired through the imagination. *Fikr* is a quality possessed only by man, and even though it is one of the means through which he can obtain knowledge of Allah, ultimately, True Knowledge of the Absolute comes through unveiling, opening, taste, insight, and witnessing.

firasa: Clear Sight. Perspicacity or clear sightedness.

ghafla: Negligent. To be negligent or heedless or unconscious of Allah. From the viewpoint of the higher teaching, *ghafla* indicates a state which, at times, may overcome some of the lesser knowers. In this state they succumb to such a state of heedlessness as to utter phrases which should be kept concealed. Perfect spiritual courtesy (*adab*) towards Allah is preserved when the knower keeps His secret within himself.

ghawth: The Help. Within the Sufi hierarchy he is the one person who forms the focus of Allah's supervision of the world in every age. He is the hidden centre of the hierarchy of saints. He is unique and alone in his time, except when the moment has led others to seek his protection and his loving concern.

al-ghayb: The Unseen. The Mystery or the Non-Manifested or the Unseen. The Unknowable or the Mystery of Mysteries. The hadith "Nothing is like Him" refers to *al-ghayb*. It is His Incomparability. It is all that is beyond reach of our vision. *al-ghayb* is all that Allah veils from you because of you, not because of Him. To attain to the Unseen, the slave and lover is told, "Leave aside your self and come!" When he obeys, it is Allah Who Sees Allah.

ghusl: Spiritual Cleansing.

hajj: Pilgrimage to the Sacred Mosque, the House of Allah, at the Centre of Mecca. *Hajj* is the ultimate journey to the knowledge of Allah Who dwells in the secret centre of the human heart. Here the treasury of spiritual realities is to be discovered. The pilgrim travels to the Sacred Centre mounted on his spiritual resolve, his overwhelming love, and his yearning for the Beloved. Mecca is the place of the House of Allah, where the slave stands alone before his Lord. Mecca is total inwardness and bewilderment. Mecca is Reality. After performing the *hajj* go to the grave of the Chosen One (*mustapha*). After realising the Unity of Allah, after being annihilated in Oneness, return to the Muhammadan Presence, because, once you know Allah, then you will know who *Rasulullah* is! Visit Holy Mecca and then visit Holy Medina. The Islamic pilgrimage is one of the ethics of the Sufis. It is the goal that they try to achieve. The pilgrimage of the Sufi is in a whole other category from that of the ordinary Muslim. As far as the pilgrimage to Mecca in Saudi Arabia, most perform it once in a lifetime, following the method of the Holy Prophet Muhammad ﷺ.

Of those who perform the pilgrimage numerous times, many choose to live in the neighbourhood of Mecca and maintain the highest *adab* and spiritual practices to remain there. The real pilgrimage in Sufi terminology is the continuation of seeking nearness to Allah.

halal: Lawful. This term indicates that which is lawful according to the Islamic Sacred Law (*shari'ah*). For the People of Reality, who adhere to both the inner and outer meanings of the Sacred Law, it is lawful to witness only Allah. Witnessing other-than-Allah is forbidden (*haram*).

haqiqah: Reality. Reality indicates the Essential Reality of things or the Divine Truth. It is the reality of the entity. *Haqiqah* is the negation of the effects of the slave's qualities by His Qualities, so that He is the agent through, in, and from the slave.

haram: Unlawful. That which is unlawful according to Islamic Sacred Law. When travelling towards the Unity, which is Allah, the lawful (*halal*) and the unlawful (*haram*) become unified as the veils are removed revealing the reality that all of existence is a complete and perfect manifestation of Allah.

al-Haqq: The Real or The Truth. The term *al-Haqq* and the Name Allah are synonymous because *al-Haqq* is the Reality which the Name Allah denotes. *Al-Haqq* also indicates its opposites, such as *khalq* (creation or creatures) and *batil* (falsehood or unreal). The Truth is that the Reality of Muhammad "fills" all space. The Reality of Muhammad is existence. Existence is the Reality of Muhammad.

haqq al-yaqin: Truth of Certainty. There are three stages of Certainty *illm al-yaqin* (the Knowledge of Certainty), *'ayn al-yaqin* (The Eye of Certainty), and *haqq al-yaqin* (The Truth of Certainty). When considering this triad, the Truth of Certainty could be likened to being consumed by the flames of a blazing fire after the two preliminary stages of *'ilm al-yaqin* (merely hearing a description of that fire) and *'ayn al-yaqin* (actually seeing the light of the flames of a fire). *Haqq al-yaqin* is the final stage in the ascent before attaining Real Islam. The seven levels of knowledge through which the traveller (*salik*) must pass are

Surrender, Belief, Perfection, Knowledge of Certainty, Eye of Certainty, Truth of Certainty, and unconditional surrender with Knowledge.

hayat as-sha'ur: Life of the Senses. This is the highest state of realisation of Allah. It is the seventh sense through which the entire body is spiritualised within Allah. It is the state of "seeing without eyes" and "hearing without ears" and "speaking without a tongue", etc. All the senses are activated and become operative through one sense alone. For example, when seeing one also hears and feels through the faculty of sight. Allah sees without eyes. Allah hears without ears. Allah speaks without a tongue. The Holy Prophet Muhammad ﷺ indicated this ultimate Life of the Senses when he said, "I see the same from my back as I see from my front." *Hayat as-sha'ur* is the highest level of abiding. All of the senses are Allah's.

himma: Intense spiritual resolve. This is the most powerful force contained within man. It is the sincere and dedicated application of all of one's efforts and strivings towards attaining the desired Object - Allah. The strength of this will results from its sincerity and the purity of its facing, its collectedness and its focusing on a specific matter. *Himma* is a pure, active force in the human being and is found in the origin of his creation and nature, or else it is acquired and developed later. From the point of view of it being a force, it is capable of attachment and is therefore attached in accordance with the will of its owner. If one attaches one's *himma* to the world, one achieves riches and position; if one attaches it to worship, one achieves stations and inspirations; and if it belongs to Allah, all attachments fallaway and the aspiration becomes one. *Himma* is to turn totally to the Creative Truth without saying "I can't" or, with regards to the self, "what's in it for me?" By using the means and the connections of work and the convictions of hope and to trust yourself with it totally. In the beginning, *himma* is that you have made firm your convictions towards obedience to Allah and fulfilling the promise of your repentance. It can develop from there and it is possible for the spiritual resolve to proceed through the following stages: The connection of one's heart by the real blessing that never diminishes. Swaying the self from the diminishing desires. Seriousness in seeking the Truth when there is reluctance. With regards to conduct, *himma* is 1. The desire to remain steadfast in the spiritual actions one performs. 2. With the continuation of visualision and the power of trust in Allah, by doing what you need to do, and you surrender to Him. With regards to manners, one should turn the *himma* totally towards proper behaviour in order to achieve the ultimate happiness and completeness. With regards to foundations, the *himma* will pull her owner towards the right of the Creative Truth by the power of the Grace of Allah. And the peace and tranquillity of being with Allah will not stop her owner or cool down. Through their spiritual resolve the great friends of Allah possess the power to perform miracles. Yet, due to their knowledge, their slavehood, and their perfect courtesy they refrain from exercising such spiritual resolve except when in compliance with a Divine Command. There can be no greater blessing for a human than the gift of being born into this earthly realm with the pre-eternal yearning to return to his Origin. It is the greatest gift that Allah gives to anyone. And, it is the highest luck, because this yearning, this *himma,* was established within the as yet unformed soul when it was still non-existent, though existent within the

Knowledge of Allah. The opposites become united in such a human, who, though dwelling in an earthly body of clay and decomposition, has a yearning soul, composed of the noble virtues and immortal qualities. For this Gift, the seeker will never be able to express his thanks to his Lord. He who has no spiritual aspiration or sincere will in seeking Allah in gratitude or in love cannot have an ambition to follow the Sufi Path of Friendship.

huwa: He. This is the Supreme Self, the Non-Manifest Being. *Huwa* indicates the Essence Itself which is always in the Unseen and remains in Itself Incomparable.

'ibadah: Worship and service of Allah with absolute obedience and love. Man was created to "know" Allah. Therefore, the essential meaning of *'ibadah* is Knowledge of Allah. Allah says in the Qur'an, "I created jinn and men only to worship (to know) Me" (Holy Qur'an 51:56). The Holy Prophet Muhammad ﷺ said, "Perfection (*ihsan*) is to worship (know) Allah like you see Him." *'Ibadah* should penetrate every aspect of a man's existence. The rites and rituals of Islam are the

outer forms containing the inner meanings which will enable the worshipper to become a knower.

ihsan: Perfection. Excellence or perfection or sanctifying virtue or spiritual beauty. *Ihsan* has three degrees: 1) To do the good that should be done with one's property, words, acts, and states, 2) To worship with total presence like one was actually seeing one's Lord, and 3) To contemplate Allah in all things, at all times and always. Perfection is the third rung on the seven-rung ladder of Knowledge. The seven levels of knowledge through which the traveller (*salik*) must pass are Surrender, Belief, Perfection, Knowledge of Certainty, Eye of Certainty, Truth of Certainty, and unconditional surrender with Knowledge.

'ilm: Knowledge. It is the analytical and indirect knowledge which results from investigation and study. *'Ilm* is contrasted with *ma'rifa*, the direct knowledge which occurs through the experiences of tasting (*dhawq*), opening (*fath*), and unveiling (*kashf*). Generally, this term applies to exoteric knowledge, but sometimes it indicates esoteric knowledge as with Knowledge of Certainty (*'ilm al-yaqin*).

'ilm al-yaqin: Knowledge of Certainty. There are three stages of Certainty – *'ilm al-yaqin* (The Knowledge of Certainty), *'ayn al-yaqin* (The Eye of Certainty), and *haqq al-yaqin* (The Truth of Certainty). When considering this triad, the Knowledge of Certainty occupies the first stage. It could be likened to hearing the description of a fire. It is followed by the Eye of Certainty, which is like actually seeing the light of the flames of that fire. Finally, there is the Truth of Certainty which is being consumed by the flames of that blazing fire. *Haqq al-yaqin* is the final stage in the ascent before attaining Real Islam. The seven levels of knowledge through which the traveller (*salik*) must pass are Surrender, Belief, Perfection, Knowledge of Certainty, Eye of Certainty, Truth of Certainty, and unconditional surrender with Knowledge.

imam: Leader of Prayer. The *imam* is "the one who is followed." When the heart has been purified through spiritual endeavour and love of Allah it becomes worthy of being the place which will contain Allah. Such a heart is the real *imam*, the truthful leader, who is to be followed in the prayer. The sanctified heart has the means to guide and lead the intellect to Knowledge of Allah. Khidr, the Green Prophet عَلَيْهِ السَّلَام is likened to the heart and the Prophet Musa عَلَيْهِ السَّلَام is likened to the intellect. Khidr عَلَيْهِ السَّلَام said, "Truly you will not be able to have patience with me. And how can you have patience about things about which your understanding is not complete?" (Holy Qur'an 18:76-68). When the heart leads the intellect, albeit momentarily, then True Knowledge of Allah descends into that heart.

islam: Surrender. The Journey of Return to Allah is from the first *islam* which is merely verbal submission, through the levels of ascent to the second and real *islam*, which is total and unconditional surrender with knowledge and love to the Will of Allah. The seven levels of knowledge through which the traveller (*salik*) must pass are Surrender, Belief, Perfection, Knowledge of Certainty, Eye of Certainty, Truth of Certainty, and unconditional surrender with Knowledge.

ism al-Jami'ah: The Name that gathers together all the Divine Names.

itlaq: Nondelimitation or Infinity.

kalimah: The Word of Faith or the Islamic declaration of Faith: "There is no god other than Allah, Muhammad is the Messenger of Allah" (*La ilaha il Allah, Muhammadan Rasulullah*).

khalifah: The viceregent of Allah is the perfected human being who has fulfilled his reason for being. He has carried the Trust which Allah offered to him, the Trust of being the locus of manifestation for the Name "Allah." The viceregent is the Perfect Man in whom Allah contemplates His own Name-derived Perfection. No one is called khalifah except through the perfection of the Divine Form within him. It is through His khalifah that Allah enters the world.

khawatir: Incoming Thoughts. These are either praiseworthy or blameworthy (divine, spiritual, ego-centric, or satanic). The Spiritual Master possesses the science of *khawatir,* and therefore knows the source of his *murid's khawatir*. He supplies the correct spiritual medicine which will restore his *murid's* health. The Word of Allah descends firstly as

Revelation (*wahy*), secondly as Inspiration (*ilham*), and thirdly as incoming thoughts (*khawatir*). *Khawatir* come to the heart from the Angelic Realm.

khawf: Fear. Fear acts as a warning of something terrifying in the future. In the initial stages of the spiritual journey the *murid* experiences great fear of the treachery of his own self and the fear of falling short of his Murshid's directions. However, when this fear is complimented with hope the *murid* finds the courage and the strength with which to attack the inner enemies. Fear of Allah leads to Knowledge of Allah which opens into Love of Allah. The lover who has found Allah fears losing Allah. Such a fear may overcome the lover who has found Allah in ecstasy during the *sama'*.

latifa: Subtle Centre. This term generally refers to the subtle essences (or centres) in the body. The cleansing of the subtle centres forms the spiritual struggle of the path. The cleansing of each separate *latifa* marks a stage in the journey of return.

ma'rifa: Divine Knowledge. It is a light which Allah casts into the heart of whomsoever He Wills. This is the true knowledge which comes through unveiling, witnessing, and tasting. This knowledge is from Allah, it is not Allah Himself because He Is Unknowable in His Essence. The triad on the Sufi path of return is comprised of fear, knowledge, and love. Fear leads to knowledge which leads to unconditional love of Allah. It is said that spiritual struggle is child's play while *ma'rifa* is men's work.

mahasin: Kindness.

maqam: Spiritual Station. A spiritual station is acquired and earned through the effort and sincerity of the traveller, but such an acquisition is ultimately through the Grace of Allah. A station is a fixed quality of the self, in contrast to the fleeting nature of a spiritual state (*hal*). When the traveller ascends to a higher *maqam* he does not leave the lower one but rather he travels with it. Once the noble qualities pertaining to a specific station are acquired, they become firmly fixed and remain with him in his endless ascent.

mukaffaf: The holding of the hand.

mu'min: Believer. The believer or the one with faith (*iman*). On the seven rung ladder to Knowledge of Allah, the believer occupies the second rung, that of *iman*. Such a believer is now safe from the hellfire, but his ascent to the Divine Presence still reaches above him. From the stage of *mu'min* he then endeavours to attain the spiritual virtues of *ihsan* and become a *muhsin*.

muqaddam: The one brought forward. One who is invested with the authority of the Shaykh. The *muqaddam* has the authority to initiate new seekers into his *tariqa* and to give them spiritual work.

muqarrabun: Those who are brought close or near to Allah and are His favoured friends. *Muqarrabun* are those perfect slaves who know that "the Lord is the Lord and the slave is the slave." They have beautiful moral courtesy with Allah, never overstepping the limits of their own limitedness and slavehood. Their love of, and devotion to, Allah is total. They see nothing but Allah. They see Allah before, in, with, and after the creation. They are the pure followers of the Holy Prophet Muhammad ﷺ. They endeavour always to emulate his perfection and in so doing they cling to their own slavehood as he did. For all this Allah draws them nearer to Himself in each moment. Their Bliss is never-ending because they dwell perpetually in His Presence. They are the People of Solitude – His perfect slaves, lovers, and knowers. He guards them through His jealousy for them. They are not known except by those who are also brought near.

muraqabah: Concentration. This term applies to the vigilant concentration, with all the power of mind, thought, imagination, and examination through which the slave carefully keeps guard over himself. During his *muraqabah* the slave observes how Allah becomes manifest both in the cosmos and within himself.

murid: Seeker. The one who desires Allah. The *murid* is the seeker of Reality who is under the direction of a Spiritual Guide (*Murshid*). He has entered the company of those who concentrate upon Allah through the remembrance of His Most Holy Name "Allah."

Murshid: Spiritual Guide. The *Murshid* is a true inheritor of the Holy Prophet Muhammad ﷺ. After having been taken to the Divine Presence during his ascension the slave has been returned, by Allah, to the creation to guide and perfect the still imperfect ones. He was taken up as a slave and returned as a slave and *Murshid*. The qualities of an authentic *Murshid* are those of his own Master and Teacher, the Holy Prophet ﷺ himself. The sacred connection between a *Murshid* and his *murids* was established in pre-eternity and continues into eternity. Because of the *Murshid's* own spiritual attainments, his *murids* have the possibility of becoming travellers. The perfect *Murshid* is of the people of blame and his *murids* sometimes also attain perfection. For the *murid*, the *Murshid* is one of the "signs on the horizons," the outward of his own inward. What he sees in the mirror of his *Murshid* is a reflection of what is within his own self. He may also see within the *Murshid* the good qualities and excellent character traits which are yet latent in himself.

nafs: The ego or the self or the soul. The *nafs* is that dimension of man which stands between the spirit which is light, and the physical body which is darkness. The spiritual struggle or combat is waged against the downward-pulling tendencies of the *nafs* which seduce the heart away from Allah. The *nafs* is also the domain of imagination. Allah is within our own selves, yet we do not see Allah. The work of the higher teaching is directed towards transforming the lower-self into the higher perfect-self and "seeing" Allah everywhere. There are seven stages of the self, seven postures in the ritual prayer, seven verses or "signs" in the opening chapter of the Qur'an, and seven levels of knowledge, all of which are finely interconnected. Shaykh Mahmoud Taha of Sudan writes concerning the self: "This soul is immortal in essence despite the changes that befall it through different forms and at different times and places. At no time does the soul cease its quest for immortality - to be immortal in form as it is in essence. This story is ... the story of every human being. However, we all have forgotten it. By 'forgetting' it is meant that it settled at the bottom of the unconscious and was then covered by a thick layer of illusions and fears that we inherited from the times of ignorance and superstition. There is no way that we can achieve our happiness unless we break through this thick layer ... which prevents the forms of the unconscious to be reflected in the mirror of the conscious and hence reveal the greater truth, the truth of truths that is shrouded by the veils of light. This long story that flows from the unconscious is made of the same stuff as that of dreams. The Qur'an is made of the same stuff. It was brought into existence only to remind us of our extraordinary story. He who remembers it will acquire knowledge beyond which there is no ignorance and an immortality beyond which there is no perishing."

nafs al-ammarratan bi su': Commanding Self. The Qur'an refers to this self, "the (human) soul is certainly prone to evil" (Holy Qur'an 12:53). This self resides in the world of the senses and is dominated by earthly desires and passions. The initial struggle in the early stages of the spiritual journey is against the Commanding Self. *Nafs al-ammarratan bi su'* is equated with the first *islam* and the first standing posture of the ritual prayer. The Commanding Self is journeying to Allah.

nasihah: Sincere advice.

nawab: Representative.

nujaba: The Nobles. Within the Sufi hierarchy these are the forty Nobles who are occupied with carrying the weight of Creation. They are not free to act except on behalf of the "other-than-Allah."

nuqaba: The Examiners. Within the Sufi hierarchy the Examiners are those who draw the hidden things out of people's selves.

qutb: The Pole. The Pole or the Pivot or the Axis. Within the Sufi hierarchy the *qutb* occupies its peak. He is the one person in every era who forms the focus of Allah's supervision of the world. The Holy Prophet Muhammad al-Mustapha ﷺ has always been, and will always be, the Beautiful Axis around whom revolve the celestial-spheres.

al-Raheem: The Merciful. One of the Beautiful Names of Allah.

al-Rahman: The Compassionate. One of the Beautiful Names of Allah.

rakat: One cycle of prayer. Each *rakat* is made up of seven movements.

ruh: Spirit. The *ruh* is that centre within man which is attracted and drawn back to its Source. The spirit endeavours to pull the heart towards Allah, while the lower-self exerts a downward pull on the heart. The human spirit is also Allah's Spirit because Allah breathed His Spirit into man. In being both uncreated and created, the *ruh* makes its descent. On the Night of Power, "therein descend the angels and the Spirit, by Allah's permission" (Holy Qur'an 97:4). The uncreated spirit is equated with the Reality of Muhammad ﷺ and the created spirit extends from the Divine Throne down to the Perfect Man. The *ruh* cannot be seen except by the man who has outstripped "both the worlds." The spirit is neither within nor without the body, neither detached from it nor attached to it. It is both within and without, detached and attached. The luminosity which radiates from a man depends upon the degree of activity of his *ruh*.

safa: Purity. The higher teaching is Purity. The word Sufi derives from *safa*. The Sufi is the slave of Allah whose self, heart, spirit, and secret have been purified, through the Remembrance of Allah, through sincere spiritual endeavour and ultimately by Allah's Grace. His heart has become the dwelling place of Allah. He is the perfect locus of manifestation for the All-Comprehensive Name "Allah." An indication to the purification of the self from the human qualities.

salat: Prayer. It refers particularly to the ritual prayer. It is a connection between the slave and his Lord. The ritual ablution which precedes the *salat* symbolises the separation from the self. The *salat* itself symbolises the joining to Allah. The seven bodily postures of the ritual prayer are symbols of the stages on the spiritual journey of return to the Source and also the seven levels of knowledge through which the traveller (*salik*) passes on his ascent. As "the one who performs the prayer" (*musalli*) approaches closer to Allah, the more profound and intense is his salat. The Holy Prophet Muhammad ﷺ said, "The prayer without you is better than seventy." As his heart is purified through spiritual struggle and the remembrance of Allah, and as he journeys along the path of return, the traveller leaves his lower-self behind. Initially the Divine Light radiates into the heart of the *musalli/salik*. Gradually this Light increases and spreads, and eventually, through the Infinite Grace of Allah, it infuses and permeates every atom of his being. Then does he pray a prayer which is without himself, because "none worships Allah but Allah."

salik: The traveller or wayfarer. The murid in a tariqa who has the necessary qualifications for spiritual travel from his lower self, through the various spiritual stations, to his Higher Self and Unity, is a *salik*. Not all members of a tariqa are travellers (*salikun*). Some are content with the blessings of being connected to the spiritual chain and feel no intensity of need to travel. The qualifications for travel were established in pre-Eternity when each non-existent entity was given its own particular preparedness to receive Knowledge of Allah.

al-Shafi: The One who gives healing. One of the Beautiful Names of Allah.

shahadah: The *shahadah,* or declaration of faith, is *Laa ilaha il Allah, Muhammadan Rasul Allah* (There is no god other than Allah, and Muhammad is the Messenger of Allah). This declaration, witnessed by two people, marks a person's entry into Islam.

shari'ah: Sacred Law. *Shari'ah* makes manifest the Divine Reality (*haqiqa*). It provides all the principles and means for a human to develop true knowledge and acquire the noble character traits. Those who know Allah never leave His Sacred Law. Their courtesy towards Allah preserves them from letting the Scale of the Law slip from their hands.

silsilat: Spiritual Chain. The spiritual chain of each *tariqa* descends from the Holy Prophet Muhammad himself ﷺ down to the present-day Shaykh. It is through his attachment to the *silsilat* that the newly initiated *murid* has the means to travel to Allah under Divine Protection.

sirr: Secret. The secret or mystery is a subtle substance of Allah's Grace. It is the innermost consciousness, the point of secret communication between the Lord and His slave. It is the hidden place where Allah manifests His mystery to Himself.

sufi: Purified One. The name *Sufi* applies to the man or woman who has purified his heart through the remembrance of Allah, travelled the path of return to Allah, and arrived at True Knowledge. There are many seekers of wisdom and Truth, but only the realised one, whose search was solely for Allah, deserves the name *Sufi*. Yet paradoxically, the one deserving of the name would never deem himself worthy of such an honour. Because he has attained such a high degree in his knowledge of Allah he knows, with certainty, that "the slave is the slave and the Lord is the Lord."

suhba: Companionship. This term applies most specifically to the spiritual relationship which exists between the *Murshid* and his *murid*. The basis of such companionship is mystical conversation and communion, both of which intensify as the *murid*'s heart becomes purified under the *Murshid*'s guidance. It is a profound mutual love based on the Pure Love of Allah.

sunnah: Practice of the Holy Prophet ﷺ. The profound science of beautiful moral behaviour based upon the beautiful model of the Holy Prophet Muhammad ﷺ. Following the form of, and contemplating the meaning within, the *sunnah* are the most profound ways in which man can prepare himself to receive Divine Knowledge.

sura: Form. The outer form of an entity or thing is what conceals its inner meaning. Revelation is the outer form whose meaning is Allah's Knowledge of Himself and His creation. Tearing away the veil of form to reveal the meaning within is the work of the higher teaching. The Holy Prophet Muhammad al-Mustapha ﷺ prayed, "O Allah, show me things as they are in their reality."

tabarruk: To receive the spiritual blessings (*baraka*).

talqin: Teach. To teach or explain a point. In *tasawwuf, talqin* is used when the Shaykh or *Murshid* says something and the *murid* repeats it back to him. This may be used when one enters Islam at the hand of the Shaykh or when entering upon the path of Allah during *bay'ah*. This practice involves a transmission of spiritual energy or *baraka* and can activate certain spiritual work for the *murid* as well. In general usage, *talqin* is also used at the burial of a Muslim. One person stays behind to remind them and to help them with the answers to the questions – Who is your Lord? Who is your Prophet? and What is your religion. This is called *talqin al-mayyit,* instructing the dead.

tanazzulat: The descent of Being by means of the Divine Revelation. This is the descent of the Absolute from Total Inwardness, through various degrees, to Outward Manifestation. The beautiful *Hadith Qudsi* says, "I was a Hidden Treasure and I loved to be known and so I created the creation, and then I became known." Man's descent through the Five Presences, from inward non-manifestation within the Knowledge of Allah to outward manifestation within the world is known as "the spiritual ascent of composition" (*'uruj al-tarkib*). His Return Journey back through the Five Presences to Allah is known as "the spiritual ascent of decomposition" (*mi'raj al-tahlil*). The Divine Revelation makes Its Decent (*tanazzulat*) in order for man to ascend along that Pure Radiation of Divine Light back to the Sacre Source. "Allah took a handful of His Light and said to it 'Be Muhammad!' and it was." The descent (*tanazzulat*) of Being is through the Holy Prophet Muhammad himself ﷺ, through his Reality (*al-haqiqah al-Muhammadiyyah*). The ascent to Being is through the Holy Prophet Muhammad, may Allah bless him and give him Eternal Peace.

tariqa: Path. It is the narrow and steep spiritual path to Reality. The qualified seeker can travel this path only under the direction of a qualified Spiritual Guide. The name *tariqa* is specific to the Islamic spiritual path.

tasawwuf: Higher Teaching. Also known as the science of the self, *tasawwuf* is based upon the teachings of the Holy

Prophet Muhammad ﷺ. It is known in the West as Sufism or Islamic mysticism. *Tasawwuf* is the acquisition of the noble character traits through purification of the heart. *Tasawwuf* is spiritual and moral courtesy (*adab*). The one who aspires to Knowledge of Allah is called a *mutasawwif*. The purified one who has made the journey of return, from his lower-self to his higher-self, is a *Sufi*. The perfect *Sufi*, who is unknown to others, is from the people of blame. The master of the people of blame, the *Sufis*, the ones who aspire, the believers and the non-believers, is the Holy Prophet Muhammad ﷺ. *Tasawwuf* is the science which takes the traveller through the unending degrees of knowing Allah. Our Master Muhammad ﷺ, the chosen one, is the means by which his followers, lovers, and slaves may attain to Allah Almighty. The manifestation of good manners outwardly is an indication to good manners inwardly as the Holy Prophet ﷺ said, "If his heart is in a state of submission then his limbs will follow suit."

tasbih: Glorification. *Tasbih* is to glorify Allah by declaring His Incomparability (*tanzih*). Allah cannot be glorified through a positive quality because "nothing is like unto

Him." *Tasbih* is closely connected to *tanzih*. The Qur'an says, "Glory be to Allah (He is) above what they ascribe (to Him)!" (37:159).

'ubudiyya: Slavehood. This is the state of the slave who is drawing near to Allah through acts of devotion. *'Ubudiyya* is "the Nearness of Supererogatory Works" (*qurb al-nawafil*), which is the lowest of the four stations of perfection. The lover/knower/slave of Allah becomes adorned with the attributes of slavehood (*'ubudiyya*) and servitude (*'ubuda*) after having lost himself in annihilation in Allah (*fana' fillah*). In becoming "no thing" (*la shay*) the slave is returned to the creation with the perfection of servitude (*'ubuda*).

wajtanibu: To shun.

warid: An inrush of knowledge and awareness. Every affair which enters the heart from any Divine Name is called a *warid*. During the collective *dhikr* and spiritual audition of the *Sufi* gatherings the one who remembers may be opened to powerful inrushes of knowledge and awareness. The effect of the inrush depends upon the preparedness and capacity to receive it. The great friends of Allah, those whose capacity is great, can receive a constant flow of these inrushes without the onlooker perceiving any external change.

wasi: Caretaker. In general usage, this word is similar to the executor of a will or bequest. In *tariqa,* this title is given as a direct appointment by the Shaykh to one who is responsible for looking after the affairs of the *zawiyya* and endeavouring to bring success to the Centre. It is the higher manifestation of the Trustee-ship (of the *wakeel*) of the *zawiyya* and contains tremendous blessing and baraka from above. As Allah said, "And this very thing did Abraham bequeath (*wasa*) unto his children, and [so did] Jacob: 'O my children! Behold, Allah has granted you the purest faith; so do not allow death to overtake you except in a sate of (the higher) Islam'" (Holy Qur'an 2:132). The *wasi* and the *wakeel* are very closely related, but *wasi* is of a higher ranking and carries with it tremendous blessing and responsibility.

wilaya: Sainthood. *Wilaya* is the sainthood of the great friends of Allah (*awliya*). It is a Divine gift and the height of human perfection. The distinguishing mark and basis of sainthood is gnosis, not holiness or piety. The friend upon whom sainthood is bestowed has no choice in this. All is the Grace of Allah. The degree of his knowledge of Allah, through which his sainthood descended, is also a gift from Allah. *Wilaya* is privacy with Allah. This privacy is indicated in the words of Muhammad al Mustapha ﷺ, "There is a time for me with Allah, in which neither the nearest angel nor a sent Prophet is contained." *Wilaya* is "seeing Allah through Allah." The friends of Allah, those upon whom wilayah has been bestowed, open up what the Prophets left closed. They are the mouthpieces of the Prophets. Through them the fragrant musk and the sweet honey of the teaching of the Holy Prophet Muhammad ﷺ continues to fill the world. Within *wilaya* there is a hierarchical order at whose peak is the Pole.

wali: Friend of Allah. He is a Sufi saint. He is the one whom Allah has chosen as His friend. The *wali* is under Allah's dome, and nobody knows him except Allah. If any among the commonality declares war upon one of Allah's friends, then Allah declare war upon that person.

wudhu: Ablution. This is the ritual ablution that all Muslims perform before entering the prayer and is unique to Islam. The literal meaning of the word (*wu-dhu*) is "to turn on the light." This "turning on the light" is the first step to entering the room. The Holy Prophet ﷺ said, "On the Day of Resurrection, my followers will be known from the traces of ablution and whoever can increase the area of his radiance should do so." By performing the ablution in the proper manner, one increases his radiance and illumination (*dhu'*), thus becoming "light upon light."

yaqin: Certainty. Allah Almighty says in the Qur'an, "and worship thy Lord until certainty comes" (Holy Qur'an 15:99). Man does not come to Certainty. Certainty comes to man. Man must actively seek Allah, but he must passively receive whatever Allah Wills to send to him.

zakat: Compulsory tax.

zawiyya: The transmission of the Divine Wisdom which flows from the *Murshid* to his *murid*s traditionally takes place in a space or room or building, which is set aside specifically for that sacred purpose. Such a place is called a *zawiyya,* which literally means "corner." The necessity for such a special place is self-evident. The *Murshid,* upon whom so many *murid*s depend to learn of the signs of the Prophet Muhammad ﷺ, needs to make himself available to them as much as possible. This meeting place, frequented as it is by numerous spiritual people, will rapidly develop into a site of highly concentrated *baraka*. An ideal *zawiyya* contains not only its own mosque, or room selected for prayer and gatherings of *dhikr,* but also larger meeting rooms for the sharing of food, both earthly and celestial. Small chambers for murids to enter spiritual retreat is of paramount importance, where the *Murshid* supervises and watches over individual *murid*s as they undergo arduous and demanding periods of seclusion. It is during such times that immense advances are made along the Spiritual Path. Just as Allah Almighty chooses to elevate certain people amongst His creation, by filling their hearts with pure love of Allah and turning them towards His remembrance, so too does Allah elevate certain pieces of His earth. Such sites are destined to become Holy places, where mosques are built, *zawiyyas* are erected or where sanctified people live in His Remembrance. The *baraka* which accumulates around and emanates from these parts of Allah's vast earth eventually attracts the pious believers and yearning lovers of Allah. These places become Sacred visiting places.

www.ingramcontent.com/pod-product-compliance
Ingram Content Group UK Ltd.
Pitfield, Milton Keynes, MK11 3LW, UK
UKHW021430280726
14060UKWH00001BA/3